In the Beginning

An Old Testament
Activity Book

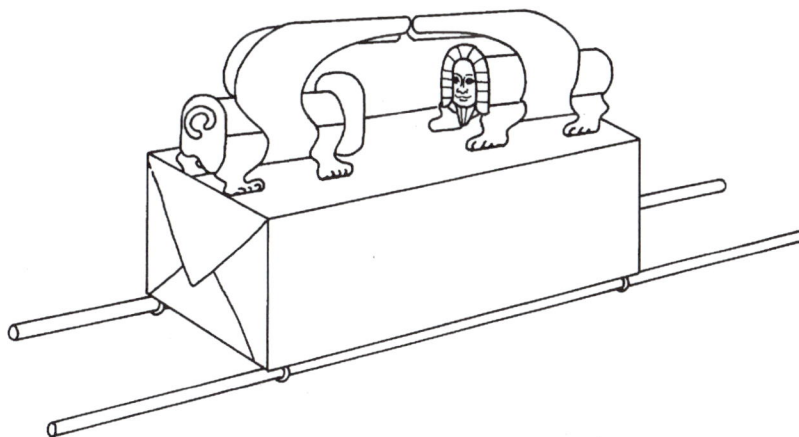

In the Beginning
An Old Testament Activity Book

Nicola Currie and Jean Thomson

Illustrated by
Julie Baines

National Society/Church House Publishing

National Society/Church House Publishing
Church House
Great Smith Street
London
SW1P 3NZ

ISBN 0 7151 4861 3

First published in 1995 by The National Society and Church House Publishing

Acknowledgements
The authors and publisher acknowledge permission to reproduce copyright material in this book. Every effort has been made to trace and contact copyright holders. If there are any inadvertent omissions we apologise to those concerned.

Bible quotations are from *The Revised Standard Version* (RSV), © 1946, 1952, 1971 by the Division of Christian Education of the National Council of Churches of Christ in the USA. Scriptures quoted from the *Good News Bible* (GNB) published by The Bible Societies/HarperCollins Publishers Ltd., UK © American Bible Society 1966, 1971, 1976, 1992, used with permission; *New English Bible* (NEB) © Oxford University Press and Cambridge University Press 1961, 1970. Material from *The Alternative Service Book 1980* is reproduced by permission of the Central Board of Finance of the Church of England. Thanks are also due to Joan Chapman for her moving fish suggestion in the chapter on Jonah and to the Council of Christians and Jews for their help on the chapters on Passover and Queen Esther.

British Library Cataloguing-in-Publication Data
A catalogue record for this book is available from the British Library.

Cover artefacts supplied by the National Society's London RE Centre
Cover design by Julian Smith
Page design and typesetting by Church House Publishing
Printed in Great Britain by Latimer Trend and Co. Ltd., Plymouth

Contents

Introduction

The rich treasury of Old Testament literature is often presented to children in story form, but there is a shortage of resources which explore the universal themes of these ancient and sacred texts. This activity book is designed to 'open up' the Old Testament for the under-11s by involving children in the stories in a variety of imaginative and practical ways.

In the Beginning encourages children to take part in the Israelites' great journey of faith. Here they can walk with Abraham, shout with Joshua and dance with King David. They can also bake unleavened bread, weave Samson's hair, create a Goliath skittle and make a salt dough lion. *In the Beginning* has hundreds of creative ideas and suggestions for the busy children's leader.

HOW TO USE THIS BOOK

The book is designed so that each chapter or story is a self-contained unit. Each chapter contains:

- **A story summary** with Biblical references.

- A list of **themes** highlighting some of the themes in the story which will be used in the activities.

- **ASB links**
  Some of the stories are in the *Alternative Service Book 1980* Sunday lectionary for Holy Communion. To help those groups who follow the lectionary these are indicated in the chapter. A complete list of the Sunday Old Testament readings covered in the book is contained in the final appendix.

- **Activities**
  Each activity suggestion gives discussion ideas, a list of the materials needed and easy-to-follow instructions with diagrams.

- **Worship**
  The book provides suggestions for worship using material discussed or created in the activity section. There are also prayer and song suggestions. The extensive number of song and hymn books available compels the authors to restrict their references to the following books:

  Junior Praise (JP)

  Songs of Fellowship (SOF)

  Come and Praise (CP)

  The English Hymnal (EH)

  Hymns Ancient and Modern New Standard (AMNS).

Age range

Each chapter is packed with activity ideas for different age groups: **younger children** broadly 5-7 year olds; **older children** 7-11 year olds and **all age** which contains material relevant to different age groups. Many of the activities can be adapted for use with different age groups.

Story-telling

Many of the activities are centred on a retelling of the story in drama, music, or mime. Leaders will find that they are able to interchange story-telling ideas between chapters. So for those chapters which are based on a 'good dramatic story' e.g. Joseph, Crossing the Red Sea, Joshua at Jericho, Samson, David and Goliath, Esther, Daniel, and Jonah etc., it will be possible to interchange and adapt the activity and drama ideas.

Timing

The material contained in each activity session should last at least 20 minutes.

Creation: In the beginning
Genesis 1-2

Themes

God is creator
The themes of the creation stories are that the earth and all that is in it belong to God. What God creates is good.

People are made in God's image
God created humanity in his image. People have a special relationship with God which is open and trusting.

Stewardship of the earth
Adam and Eve were given a special responsibility by God to look after the earth. For children the stories provide a religious framework for work on the environment, nature study and appreciation and care of the earth.

ASB links
9 before Christmas
Years One and Two

Bible quotation
Then God said, 'Let us make man in our image and likeness to rule the fish in the sea, the birds of heaven, the cattle, all wild animals on earth, and all reptiles that crawl upon the earth.'
Genesis 1 v26, NEB

The stories of creation in the first two chapters of Genesis show God as the creator of the universe. Poetically they describe how the ancient writers believed the world came into existence. God created the world out of nothing. He created the heavens and the earth; darkness and light; the seas and dry land; the plants and trees; the stars, sun and moon; the fish, animals and all living creatures and finally he created people. Humankind was made in God's image and was given responsibility for what God had created. All that God had made was good.

ACTIVITIES

Younger children

The beauty of creation
This activity is designed to help children appreciate the beauty of the world in their immediate environment.

You will need
drawing materials
paper

Take the children outside into a park, churchyard, field or garden and ask them to do one of the following activities for two minutes:

* Pick a flower and look at it carefully.
* Lie down on the grass and with their eyes closed listen carefully and feel all around.
* Look very carefully under a small stone.

Discussion
Ask the children about what they have seen and heard. Encourage the group to describe the beauty of what they have seen and heard and the intricacy of the world around them.

An alternative activity for indoors
Take a selection of natural things: leaves, flowers, stones, shells etc. into the group. Encourage the children to look carefully, feel

and smell the objects. If possible let them look at the objects through a magnifying glass.

Discussion
Ask them to describe in words or pictures the beauty of what they have found.

The beauty of creation

You will need

For activity 1	For activity 2
greaseproof paper	*black sugar paper*
felt-tip pens	*scissors*
Blu-Tack	*glue*
	coloured tissue paper
	* or cellophane*
	Blu-Tack

Read the story of creation to the group and ask them to shut their eyes and imagine the Garden of Eden. They can recreate their imagined paradise by making a stained glass window.

There are two different ways of making a window:

1 Give each child a sheet of greaseproof paper and ask them to draw their picture in felt-tip pens. The window tracery can be drawn with a black felt-tip pen.

2 Alternatively use a large sheet of black sugar paper and mark out the tracery. Cut this out. Stick coloured tissue paper or cellophane paper on the reverse of the paper.

Both types of window can be stuck on a window for the light to shine through.

A planned paradise

You will need
drawing materials
paper

The creation story shows how God planned and created a perfect paradise. This activity can help children appreciate the wonder of creation.

Ask the group to:

• Plan a perfect island paradise to live on.

• Draw a map of this paradise island.

• Think about what they would need to survive on an island.

• Decide who they would like to live on their island with them.

You could go on to make models of the islands but the maps provide a starting point for a discussion.

Discussion
Discuss with the children the things they have included on their islands.

• Have they thought about the need for water, food, air, light?

• Have they thought long-term or only about their immediate needs?

• Are they pleased with their plans – are their plans good or do they fail in some way?

The biblical story shows how God thought of everything. The creation he planned was good and perfect.

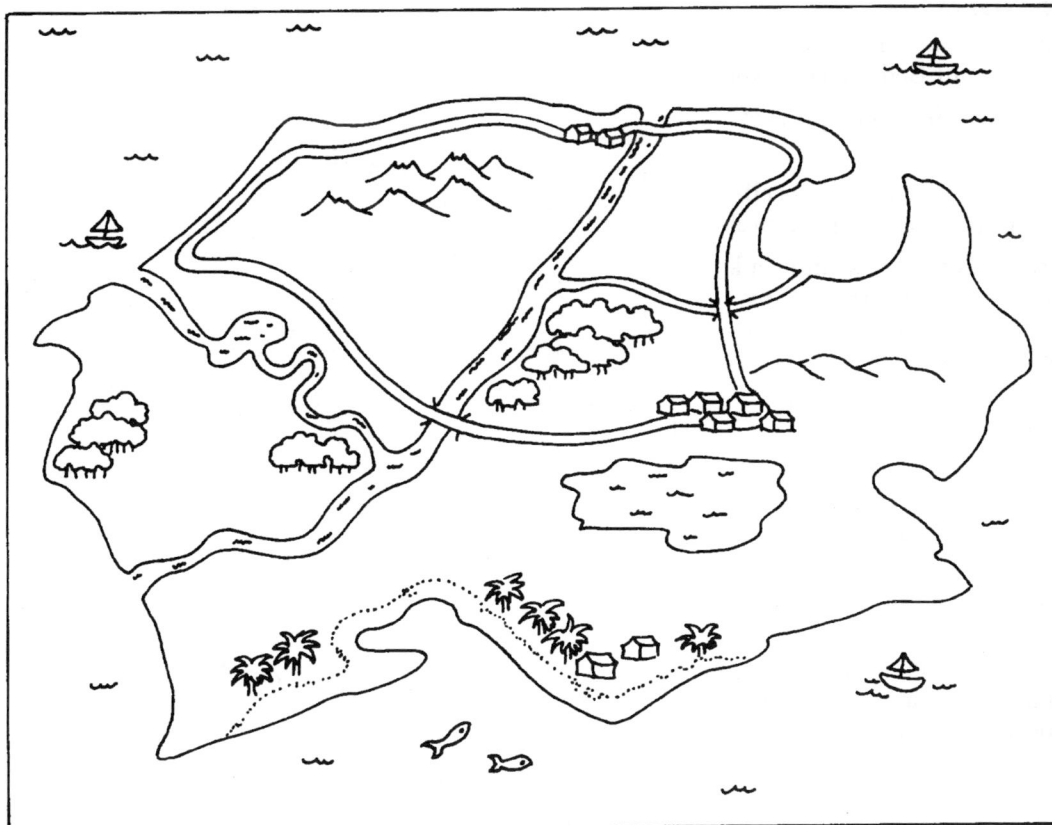

Action stations: taking care of the world

All age

You will need
drawing materials
paper

The creation story shows that people have a special responsibility to look after the world. Discuss with the children how they take care of the things around them – possessions, plants, pets, and each other.

Ask the group to draw up an action plan for caring for the earth using the word 'creation' as a starting point. Here is an example.

C Conserve fossil fuels – walk or ride a bike rather than get a lift.

R Recycle glass, paper, cans, clothes and arrange collections in your area.

E Energy saving – use energy efficient light bulbs – remember to switch things off.

A Act together and work with others.

T Transform an area of garden or waste land.

I Inform others about what you are doing and why.

O Only buy products which are environmentally friendly and do not exploit workers in the Third World.

N Never take your friends for granted.

Discuss with them how they could start to implement their action plan at home, in church and at school.

Taking care of the world: a self-portrait

This activity helps children see how people have spoilt God's perfect world.

- Draw a large circle on a piece of paper.
- The children should draw a self-portrait in the middle of the circle.
- Take the group outside and walk around slowly in a circle taking note of all that surrounds them including the rubbish and dirt as well as the trees, plants and animals.
- On your return each child should draw the things they have seen on their walk around their self-portraits.

Discuss with them the differences between the world as God first made it and the world that surrounds them now. What could they do to improve the environment around them?

WORSHIP
Theme: Giving thanks to God for creation

Prayer
Almighty God,
you have created the heavens and the earth
and made man in your own image.
Teach us to discern your hand in all your works,
and to serve you
with reverence and thanksgiving;
through Jesus Christ our Lord, who with you
and the Holy Spirit
reigns supreme over all things
now and for ever.
ASB collect for the 9th Sunday before Christmas

Song suggestions
If I were a butterfly (JP94, SOF74)
Morning has broken (CP1, JP166)
Who put the colours in the rainbow (CP12, JP288)
All things bright and beautiful
(AMNS116, CP3, EH587, JP6)
For the beauty of the earth
(AMNS104, CP11, EH309, JP48)
Long long ago (JP419)
He made me (CP18)

The Fall
Genesis 3

Themes
Temptation

The parable shows how people fall into sin and are tempted. First the seed of doubt is sown by distorting God's words. Then the tempter denies the truth of God's warning – they should not eat of the tree, not because they will die, but because they will gain wisdom. Eve believes this and her understanding of the goodness of God is shattered. She then wants what she cannot have and finally disobeys God. Doubt led to disobedience and her reason for doubt is pride, self-assertion or a hunger for power.

Sin and separation

The Fall is a story of how people became separated from God. It contains profound truths about humankind's relationship with God. The ancient writers believed that people originally lived in a full and open relationship with God. This relationship changed when sin entered the world. Sin is shown as a separation from God. The story explains how sin, or humankind's rebellion against God, destroys the relationship between people and God, between people, and between people and God's earth.

ASB links

Lent 1 in Year One and 8 before Christmas in Year Two

Did you know?

In the ancient mythology of Canaan the serpent was the symbol of the god Eshmun, who was the god of healing. A rod with an entwined serpent was the god's magic implement of healing. In Greek mythology the serpent is connected with the underworld and with reincarnation because of its power to change its skin. It was also a symbol of fertility. To the writer of Genesis the serpent with its knowledge and promises was a symbol of the guile that leads people to destruction.

Bible quotation

The woman saw how beautiful the tree was and how good its fruit would be to eat, and she thought how wonderful it would be to become wise. So she took some of the fruit and ate it.
Genesis 3 v6, GNB

The story of the Fall is an explanation by the ancient writers of how people first spoiled a perfect relationship with God. Adam and Eve had trusted in God's goodness. They lived in harmony with God, with each other and with the world God had made. Then Eve was tempted by the serpent to eat from the tree which God had forbidden them to eat from, 'You will not die. For God knows that when you eat of it your eyes will be opened, and you will be like God, knowing good and evil.' (Genesis 3 v5, RSV) Adam and Eve disobeyed God by eating the fruit from the tree. When God challenged Adam by asking him why he ate the fruit he blamed Eve and Eve in turn blamed the serpent. The relationship was spoilt, the trust was broken. Adam and Eve feared God and become separated from him. God then sent Adam and Eve out of the garden and paradise was lost.

Christians believe that Jesus restored the right relationship between God and humanity again, through his life and death.

ACTIVITIES
Retell the story of the Fall

Place two large mats at different ends of the room. One mat is the garden of Eden. Choose four children to mime the story of the Fall. The leader can retell the story of how Eve was tempted by the snake while the children mime it. When 'God' banishes 'Adam and Eve' from the garden the children have to flee to the other mat. The gap between the two mats is too large to jump back across. The child acting God then places 'paving stone' pieces of paper to the other mat. Write the letters 'JESUS' on the different 'stones'. The leader can explain that Christians believe that God sent Jesus into the world so that all people can be friends with God again.

The forbidden fruit – or trick sweets and saying we are sorry

Younger children

These activities explore how temptation tricks people into thinking something is better than it is. They also explore the theme of repentance.

You will need
one plate of plain biscuits
one plate of sweet wrappers covering dried bread pieces of paper shaped as different fruits
sweets

11

In the session the group is offered the choice of two plates.

Hopefully most children choose the dried bread 'trick sweets'. Discuss with them what they feel. Do they like being tricked? Why did they choose the sweets rather than the biscuits?

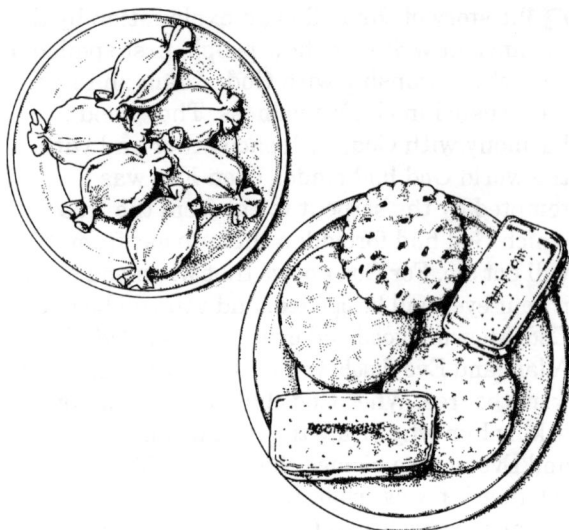

The leader should then explain that in the story of the Fall Eve believes the snake. She looks at the fruit from the forbidden tree and thinks how beautiful the tree is and how good its fruit. When she ate the fruit, she disobeyed God. She was tricked by the snake whom she had trusted. Explain that temptation is often very attractive to people, just as the lovely-looking sweets seemed attractive. The leader can now offer real sweets to all the children and apologise for tricking them.

Fruit turn-arounds
Talk with the group about how everybody does wrong things sometimes. The leader should tell a story of something they have done wrong during the week. Explain that even when people do things wrong, God still loves them and wants them to become friends with him again. But first people need to say they are sorry to God.

Hand out the paper fruit shapes to the group and ask them to:

• Think of something they have done wrong during the week.

• Illustrate this on the fruit shape.

• Draw a smiley face on the reverse of the fruit.

During the worship time the children can say sorry to God for the things they have done wrong during the week. When they have said sorry they can turn their fruits around to show the smiley faces.

Doing wrong and separation – a card slider
This activity explores the consequences of wrong-doing and how it leads to separation from people and God.

You will need
a cereal box for each child
scissors
drawing materials
a compass
a ruler

Discussion
Ask each child to think of a time in the week when they have done something wrong – disobeyed their parents or teachers, fallen out with a friend, been unfair to their siblings etc. Discuss with them the consequences of what they did. How did they feel towards the person they had done wrong to? Did it separate them from that person? Were they punished for what they did?

Activity

These card sliders illustrate how wrong-doing leads to separation.

Give each child a cereal box. The children should then

- Cut the side panels from the front and back of the packet.

- On the plain side of the front of the packet cut two vertical 5cm slits 10cm apart from each other as shown opposite.

- On one side panel cut along the dotted lines indicated below.

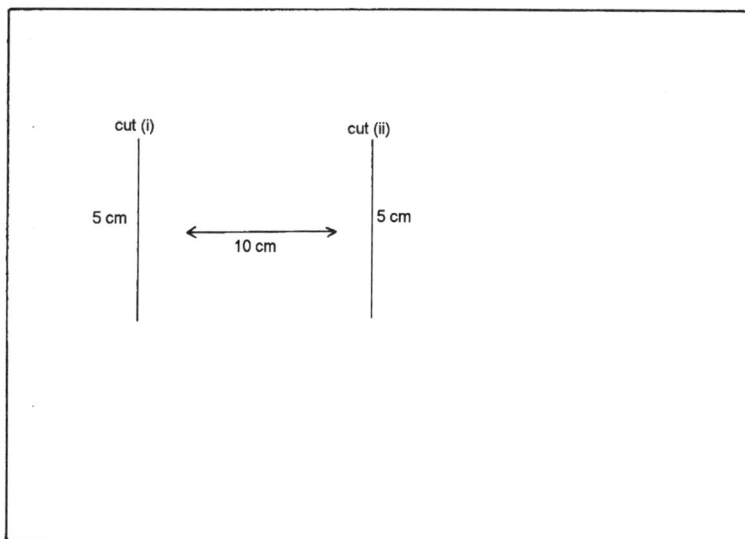

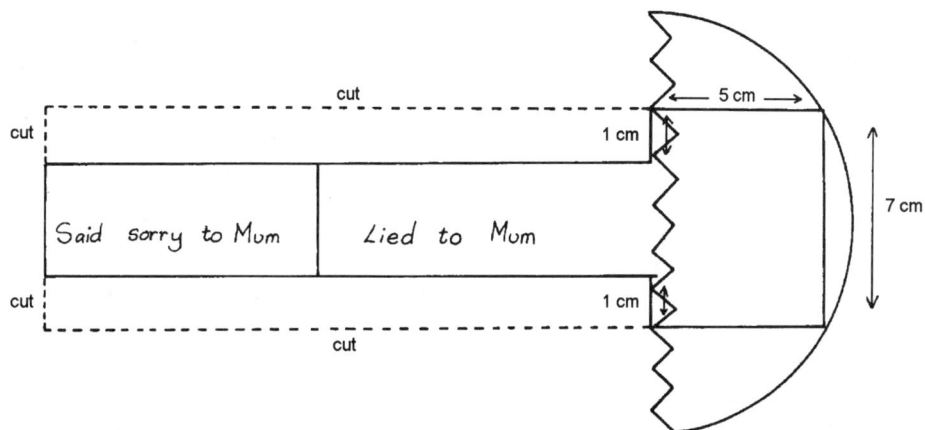

- On the back of the packet cut out a circle 12cm in diameter.

- On this circle draw a ragged line as shown below. On the right hand side draw a picture of themselves. On the left hand side draw a picture of the person they have fallen out with or done something wrong towards. Cut along the ragged line to form two sections.

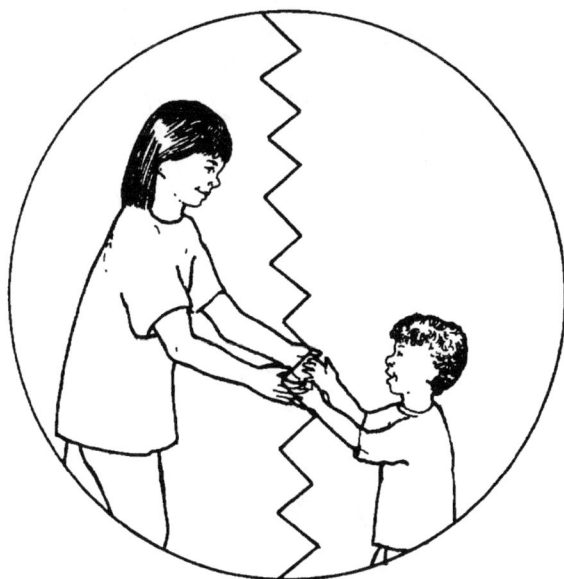

- Glue the right hand half of the circle to the side panel strip as illustrated.

- Thread the strip through slit ii) and slit i) on the large cereal packet.

- Pull the tab through so that the right hand half circle rests next to slit ii).

- Carefully glue the left hand half of the circle next to the right hand half so that they fit together to make a whole.

- Pull out the right hand half of the circle so that the tab is half out. In this space ask the children to write down the thing they did wrong.

- Pull the tab so that the half circles meet and on the space at the other end of the tab the children should write 'said sorry to . . . '

- By pulling the circles apart the children can see the separation their wrong-doing could cause.

- By pulling the tab the other way they can see how saying they are sorry can bring people together again.

After the children have played with their sliders discuss how doing wrong can separate people. Christians believe that doing wrong also separates people from God. Just as people need to say they are sorry to people they have wronged, so they also need to say sorry to God. Sometimes people cannot forgive or say they

13

are sorry but Christians believe that God is constant; he is always willing to forgive.

The consequences of sin – a snakes and ladders game

All age

This game illustrates how sin, or doing wrong separates people from God.

You will need

*a large sheet of paper divided into 100
  numbered squares (write the start and finish
  squares on the board – see illustration)*
templates of the snakes and ladders
drawing materials
scissors
glue
dice
counters

Discussion

Ask each child to think of a time when they have been tempted to do something wrong. To get the discussion going the leader might think of a story when a child has stolen something; spent all their money on something leaving none for Christmas presents; gone to a place that is forbidden or eaten something without permission. Ask the children to think what attracted the child in the story to do something wrong? What were the consequences of their actions? Now focus on the children in the group and ask them about the consequences of something they have done wrong.

Activity

Divide the children into pairs.
Each pair then

- Cuts out a snake and a ladder.

- Colours in the snakes.

- Glues the snakes between two squares on the board with the head on the upper square.

- On the upper square the children should write a temptation that leads to wrong-doing, it could be one of the things they have discussed.

- On the lower square they should write the consequences of the wrong-doing.

- Place the ladders on the board in the same way as the snakes.

- On the ladders write the word 'sorry'.

Remind the children that when they have done wrong, they

become separated from people and from God. To restore a good relationship and become friends again people need to say they are sorry.

The children can then play snakes and ladders as a reminder of the session.

WORSHIP
Theme: Saying sorry

The children can use their turn-over fruits during the worship.

Prayer

Father God, we are sorry for the things which we do wrong which separate us from you and from each other. We ask for your forgiveness and for your help through this next week to do what is right. Amen.

Song suggestions

Dear Lord and Father of mankind
(AMNS115, EH383, JP37)
Cleanse me from my sin Lord (JP27)
What a friend we have in Jesus (JP273)
Walking in the garden (AMNS518)
In Adam we have all been one (AMNS474)

Finish

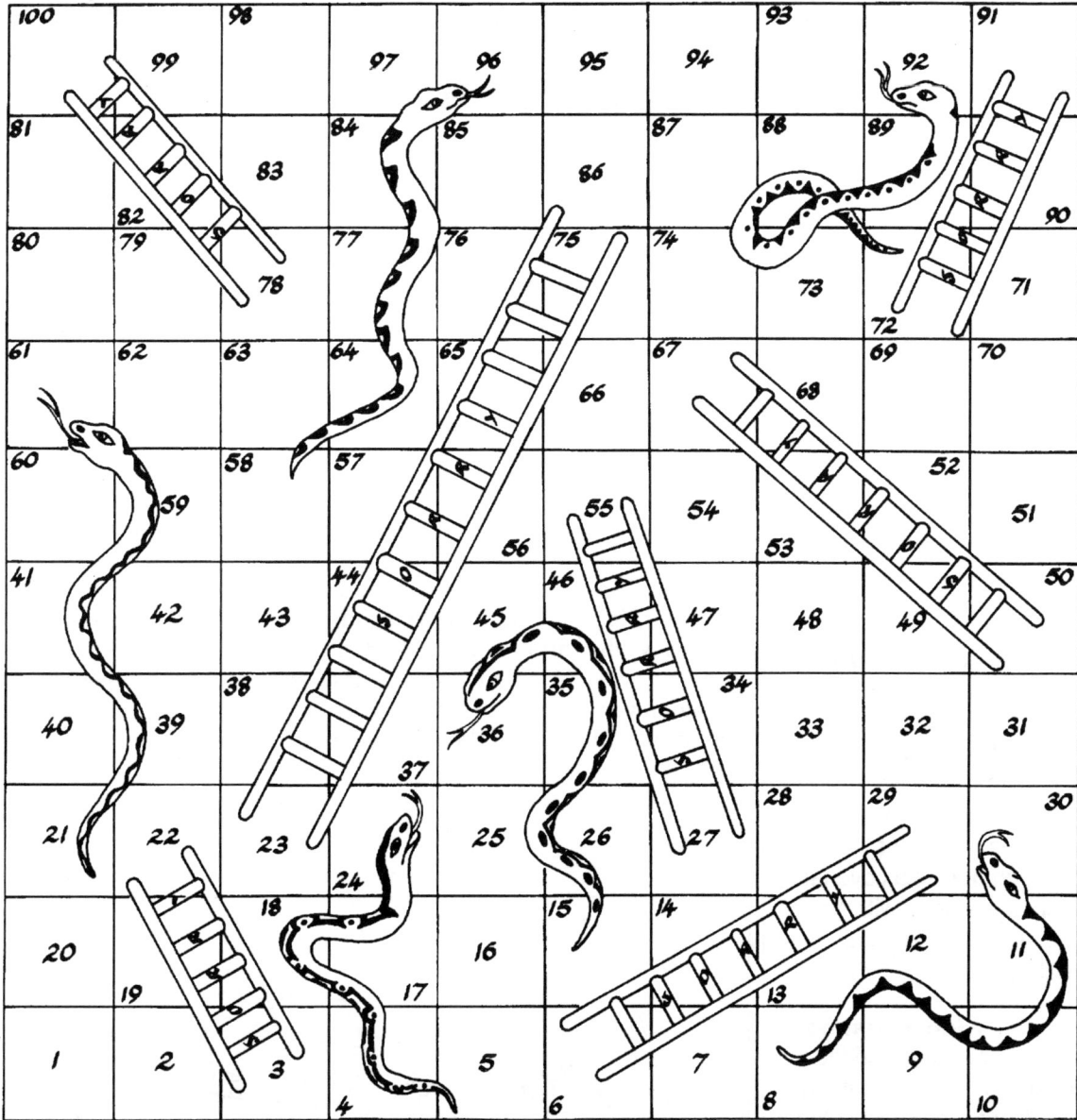

Start

Noah and the flood
Genesis 6-9

Themes

Judgement, punishment and mercy
The people of the earth had rejected God's ways and disobeyed him. God cannot let the evil and violence continue. God uses his power and judges the sin. He sends a flood to destroy all that lives on earth but has mercy on Noah, his family and the animals, and protects them.

Promises and covenant
God promises Noah that he will save him and his family and two of every kind of animal. The Noah story shows how God keeps his promises. When the flood is over God makes a covenant (an agreement) with Noah and every living creature, that he will not send a flood again.

Righteousness
Noah is described in Genesis 7 v1 as a righteous man. He was 'right' with God. He recognised God's will and kept faith with him.

ASB links
Lent 2 Years One and Two

God saw that the world was evil and full of violence. He decided to destroy the earth. But first he chose a good man, Noah, and told him to make himself an ark, giving him precise instructions about the building. God promised Noah that he and his family, two of every kind of animal, male together with female, would be saved from the destruction.

God sent a flood which covered the whole earth. The rain continued for forty days and forty nights and everything was destroyed apart from the ark.

At the end of forty days Noah sent out from the ark first a raven and then a dove to see if the waters had subsided. But the dove found nowhere to rest. After another seven days he sent the dove again and this time the dove returned with an olive leaf in its beak, showing Noah that trees were again growing. When the ark came to rest Noah built an altar to God and made a sacrifice. God made a covenant with Noah and every living creature. He promised that he would never again send a flood to destroy the world. He made a rainbow as the sign of the agreement.

ACTIVITIES

Younger children

Saving Noah and the animals
These game and drama activities illustrate how God shows mercy on Noah, his family, and the animals, because Noah is faithful.

Before the session
For the animal game, cut out pictures of animals from magazines and comics. Make sure you have two of each animal. It would be helpful to include a raven and a dove which will can be used in the play. You will also need to provide face paints.

In the session

Retell the story of Noah and the flood. Then play this animal game.

- Hand each child a picture of an animal and ask them to find the person who has the same animal.
- All the children have to make the sound or the movement their animal makes.
- The children find their partners by listening for the right sound.
- When the children have found their partners they can use the face paints to draw the faces of their animals on each other.
- The leader can be Noah and retell the story as the children act it out.

Keeping promises

Older children

God keeps his promises to those who are faithful to him. God protects them and keeps them safe. In this activity the children are reminded that Noah was protected by God and that God kept his promise.

Discussion and Bible study

- Discuss with the group what makes them feel unsafe and afraid: a storm at sea, being lost in a shop, a test at school, getting lost in a dark room or on a path, etc.
- Where do they feel most safe? At home? In their room? With friends and family?

There are many stories in the Bible which show how God protects people from the things which they most fear. Divide the group into three and ask each group to look up one of the following Biblical passages in the Good News Bible:

1 Samuel 25 v29
Psalm 23 v4
Psalm 63 v7-8

How does the writer of each passage visualise God's protection?

In the Noah story God protects Noah and his family. He gives them instructions for building an ark and when they have all entered the ark we are told 'Then the Lord shut the door behind Noah.' (Genesis 7 v16, GNB).

These points can be illustrated to the group by making a collage.

A Noah's ark collage

All age

See the illustration on the previous page.

You will need
blue and green plastic carrier bags
sticky labels or blue and green paper
clear plastic
sponges
large sheets of card
drawing materials
paper
paintbrushes
paints
glue
scissors

- To make the stormy sky, sponge paint in blue and grey on a large sheet of card or paper.
- Ask each child to make a wave shape out of a plastic carrier bag or blue or green paper. On this shape they should write down what it is they are frightened of. If you are using the plastic bags write on sticky labels and stick these to the waves.

Lion   Monkey   Frog

- Stick these waves to the background card so that they stand proud.

- Make an ark from a large sheet of card. Cut out the door as shown.

- Stick the ark onto the sea.

- Open the ark doors and ask each child to draw their face behind the door.

- To make the rain cut strips of clear plastic and attach these to the top of the picture to create an impression of pouring rain.

- Remind the children that just as God protected Noah in the ark, he protects them.

Keeping promises

All age

These activities explore what is entailed by keeping a promise.

Discussion
Ask the children

- What promises do they keep?

- Why do they keep them?

- Are some promises more difficult to keep than others?

- What helps to keep a promise?

People often break their promises but God always keeps his promises. In the Noah story God said he would make a covenant with Noah (Genesis 6 v18); he did not forget Noah (Genesis 8 v1); he promises never to destroy all living beings again (Genesis 8 v21) and puts a rainbow in the sky as a sign of his everlasting promise (Genesis 9 v16).

Promises are made between at least two people. One person makes a pledge to another. The other person trusts that the promise will be kept.

By organising a promises auction the children can appreciate more about what it means to make and keep a promise.

A promises auction
This activity can be used to raise money.
Ask the children to think of things which they can do that might be helpful to members of their family: cleaning cars, gardening, tidying a room, spring cleaning, cookery.

- They should then decide to offer one particular skill to their family.

- On a card they write – I promise to give the bearer of this certificate . . . (and then put their offer).

- The leader should then arrange a time when the children can offer their promise to their families in a public meeting.

- Different members of the family might want to bid for the promises.

- Once an agreement has been made the child signs his certificate and arranges to fulfil the promise.

This activity can be adapted for use in a congregation where adult and child members of a family work together to fulfil a promise.

WORSHIP
Theme: God's protection

Prayer
Almighty and everlasting Father,
we thank you that you have brought us safely
to the beginning of this day.
Keep us from falling into sin or running into danger;
order us in all our doings;
and guide us to do always
what is right in your eyes;
through Jesus Christ our Lord. Amen.
ASB collect for Morning Prayer

Song suggestions
Captain Noah and His Floating Zoo by Michael Flanders and Joseph Horovitz (Novello)
Mister Noah built an ark (JP167)
Noah was the only good man (JP432)
Old man Noah (JP440: suitable for very young children)
Rise and shine (JP210)
All my hope on God is founded (AMNS336)

The call of Abraham
Genesis 12 v1-9

Themes
God's promise
God promised Abraham that he would possess a land, become a great nation and that through him the people of the earth would be blessed. This three-fold divine promise runs throughout the Old Testament.

Trust
In response, Abraham completely trusted in God. He gave up his home and all that he knew and travelled to a strange and foreign land.

ASB links
7 before Christmas Year One and Lent 3 Year Two

Bible quotation
The Lord took him outside and said, 'Look at the sky and try to count the stars; you will have as many descendants as that.'
Genesis 15 v5, GNB

Abraham was the first patriarch, the first great Biblical father figure and leader of the people of Israel. The story of Abraham begins the epic of how God's people, the Jews, came to the promised land. Abraham completely trusted in God's promise to him. He left his country, his family and his father's house and travelled from Mesopotamia to Canaan. God told Abraham that he would bless him and his descendants and make him a great nation.

Today Abraham is the father figure of three religions: Judaism, Islam and Christianity.

ACTIVITIES
Retell the story of the call of Abraham to the group by doing one of these activities.

1   On three separate sheets of paper write Haran, Moreh and Southern Canaan. Before telling the story put these labels in different places in the room. Start with all the children in Haran and then tell the story while travelling with the children through Moreh to Southern Canaan.

2   Throw a blanket over a table and sit underneath. Ask the children to pretend that they are Abraham and his family living in a tent in Canaan. 'Abraham' should recount to his grandchildren how he travelled from his family home to his new home in Canaan.

Inheritors of Abraham's faith: Stars in the sky frieze

Younger children

Christians believe that they are inheritors of the promise God made to Abraham. God told Abraham that his descendants would be as many as the stars in the sky (see Bible quotation). This image can be illustrated by making a stars in the sky frieze.

You will need
black or dark blue sugar paper
yellow paper
templates for stars
scissors
pencils
glue and spreaders
crayons

Before the session

- Make a night sky from sheets of sugar paper.

- Make star templates of different sizes from enlargements of the illustrations above.

In the session

- Draw around the star templates on yellow paper. Cut the stars out.

- Write their name or ask them to draw a picture of themselves on the star. (If there are only a few members in the group, the children could do stars for members of their family or for children who are not present). The group leader should make a star as well.

- Glue the stars onto the sky background.

Talk about the completed frieze with the group. Remind them that they are inheritors of God's promise to Abraham and receive God's blessings.

'What did Abraham give up?' collages   **Older children**

When Abraham left his home he gave up his country, his people, his friends and his security because he trusted in God. This activity explores this change in lifestyle.

You will need
*old catalogues which include household and
    camping goods*
large sheets of paper
scissors
glue and spreaders
drawing materials

Before the session

- Cut out shapes of a large paper house and a large paper tent. You could use enlargements of the templates on the next page.

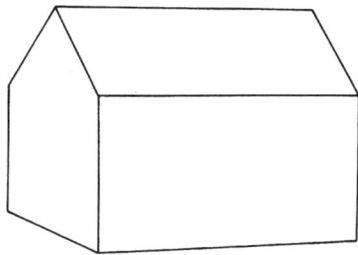

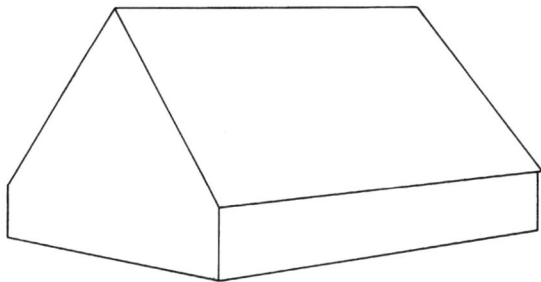

In the session

- Cut out from the catalogues items for a home and items for camping.

- Sort the pictures out and decide which ones to put on the paper house and which on the tent.

- Glue the pictures onto the house or tent.

Discussion
After the pictures have been completed put them where everyone can see them and discuss these questions.

- Are there more things for the home than the tent?

- What are the main differences between living in a house and living in a tent?

- Camping is exciting in summer but what would it be like all the year round?

- Abraham was asked by God to give up the comforts and security of living in Haran and travel to an unknown place. Have any of the group experienced moving from a place they knew and loved to a place that they did not know? What did they feel?

Like Abraham sometimes Christians believe that they have to give up something they like in order to follow the Christian life more closely. This might be giving up part of an income to give to charity, giving up time to help someone or changing a lifestyle. The leader might be able to give an example to the children of something they have felt they should give up.

'Listening to a call' games

All age

To obey God's call, Abraham needed to recognise God's voice, do as God commanded and trust in God's help. These games explore the themes of listening, obedience, trust and support.

You will need
blindfolds
drawing materials
one sheet of paper divided into four for each child (the four sections should be headed 'Trust the leader', 'Helped in difficulties', 'Recognise and listen to the caller's voice' and 'Follow directions')

Before the session
Prepare the room for an obstacle course using tables, chairs and boxes and have extra 'props' for 'Simon Says'.

In the session
The children can play these games:

1 Following the call

- Divide the group into pairs of callers and listeners.

- Put blindfolds on the listeners.

- The listeners should stand at one end of the room and the callers at the other and call directions.

- The callers have to direct the listeners over to where they are standing e.g. 'One step forward. Right five steps.'

- The leader needs to look out for any children who get into difficulties and help them out.

- If there is time, swap the callers with the listeners and play the game again.

Discussion
When the game is over ask the children to tell you what the listener has to do to get safely from one side of the room to the other. Make sure that they realise that shouting is not as important as recognising the voice, following the directions, trusting that the directions are correct and knowing that someone will help when they are in difficulty.

2 Following the leader
The adult should be the leader.

- Either ask the children to do something on the spot in the same way as 'Simon Says'. Include more complicated instructions like 'Pretend to help a friend across the road', 'Blow up a paper bag and burst it' or 'Juggle with two beanbags'. Encourage them to help one another.

- Alternatively ask them to line up behind you and do what you do as well as follow your spoken directions. Again encourage the children to help each other.

Discussion
When the game is over ask the children what helped them to keep going? Emphasise that it was important that they followed even though they did not know where they were going. They

21

needed to trust the leader, listen to the leader, follow directions and know there would be help when they got into difficulties.

On the sheets of paper ask the children to illustrate their experiences in each of the sections provided. The leader needs to draw out the connections between what the group has just learnt and the story of Abraham's trust in God.

WORSHIP

Using whatever has been done by the children, summarise what they have found out about Abraham in the session, e.g.

- He was a friend of God. When he heard God's voice, he followed God's directions, leaving the comforts of his home.

- God blessed Abraham and his descendants.

- Abraham's decendents all receive God's blessings today. Jesus promised that he would be with people always.

Prayer

Almighty God,
whose chosen servant Abraham
faithfully obeyed your call
and rejoiced in your promise
that, in him, all the families of the earth shall be blessed:
give us a faith like his,
that, in us, your promises may be fulfilled;
through Jesus Christ our Lord.
ASB 7th Sunday before Christmas

Song suggestions

Father I place into your hands (JP42, SOF31)
Father, lead me day by day (JP43)
Father Abraham (SOF29)
One more step (CP47, JP188)
Have faith in God, my heart (AMNS372)
Guide me, O thou great Redeemer
(AMNS214, EH397)
O Jesus, I have promised (AMNS235, EH577)

Joseph and his brothers
Genesis 37

Themes
Favouritism and sibling rivalry
The Joseph story is timeless. Favouritism, sibling rivalry, jealousy and revenge exist today in family relationships. Children still dislike the child who tells tales, who is favoured by a parent. The Joseph story has a happy ending. Joseph becomes a great man and he forgives his brothers.

God's choice of people
Joseph became a great man but the story of his childhood reveals that he was less than likeable. The Joseph story shows how God often uses people who are far from perfect to fulfil his plans.

ASB links
The conclusion of the story of Joseph and his brothers and their reconciliation is the reading for Pentecost 14 Year Two.

Bible quotation
When his brothers saw that their father loved Joseph more than he loved them, they hated their brother so much that they would not speak to him in a friendly manner.
Genesis 37 v4, GNB

Thanks to the Tim Rice/Andrew Lloyd-Webber musical – *Joseph and his Amazing Technicolor Dreamcoat* – the young Joseph is one of the better-known Old Testament characters.

Joseph was the favourite son of Jacob. Jacob made Joseph a fine long robe as a sign of his fondness for the boy. This gift made Joseph's brothers jealous. Joseph had two dreams which were interpreted that his family would bow down to him. This made his brothers even more angry with him and they plotted to kill their brother. One day Jacob sent Joseph to visit his brothers who were looking after the flocks. Reuben, one of Joseph's brothers, said that they should not kill Joseph but put him in a pit. The brothers caught Joseph, took his long robe from him and put him into the pit. Then a group of Ishmaelites went past them on their way to Egypt. The brothers sold Joseph to the Ishmaelites. They then covered Joseph's robe with the blood of a goat so that they could pretend to their father that Joseph had been killed.

ACTIVITIES
These activities explore the consequences of family favouritism and rivalry.

Favouritism and special gifts

Younger children

Jacob gave Joseph a special coat to wear. This coat was a sign of Jacob's favouritism of Joseph. This activity helps children understand the feelings of jealousy and rivalry Joseph's brothers had.

You will need
a box of dressing up clothes which includes one attractive costume

In the session
- Ask the children to dress up in the clothes and pretend they are the person they have dressed up as.
- Discuss any disputes or feelings of jealousy between them.
- Would they have felt jealous of Joseph?
- Would they have been annoyed by Jacob's favouritism and special gifts to Joseph?

Making a coat

This game explores what it is like to have special presents and gifts like Joseph. It also exposes the danger of boasting.

You will need
an old coat
rich and brightly coloured materials
collage materials
safety pins or sewing materials

- The children can make their own model of Joseph's coat by attaching brightly coloured materials to an existing old coat with safety pins or with needle and thread.

- Ask the group to make up their own drama of Joseph, his father and brothers.

- They should take it in turns to wear the coat and be Joseph. The other children should bow down and pay homage to Joseph, e.g. 'Your excellency, how wonderful you are looking today', 'Your highness, may I touch your royal coat?' etc. This reminds them of Joseph's dream when his brothers bowed down to him.

Discussion
After the drama discuss with the children

- What did it feel like to be Joseph?

- Did the coat make them feel great? Important? Embarrassed? Proud? Beautiful?

- Did they enjoy the position of power?

- Did they like boasting or showing off when they were Joseph?

- Why didn't Joseph's brothers like him?

The drama of family arguments

You will need
drawing materials
paper

The divisions in Jacob's family were resolved when Joseph grew up, used his special gifts in a mature way and forgave his brothers. His brothers were understandably cross that Joseph was the favourite son and had dreams that showed him ruling them. Explore sibling rivalry by discussing this story with the group:

'Kevin had been given an expensive pair of trainers by his mother. He went around the house showing off and talking about how great he felt in his new trainers. Sam his younger brother wanted a new pair too. Sam said that it wasn't fair and he took one of Kevin's trainers and drew over it with a felt-tip pen. Kevin hit his brother and Sam went crying to his mother. Their mother came in and told Kevin off.'

Discuss these questions with the group

- What could Kevin have done to prevent Sam getting so upset?

- Should Sam have scribbled on the trainers?

- If you were the boys' mother what could you have done to prevent this situation?

Try to get the group to understand the point of view of the different characters in the story.

The children can draw a cartoon strip of the story with a 'happy ending'.

WORSHIP
Theme: The need to forgive in families

Prayer
Heavenly Father,
whose blessed Son shared at Nazareth
the life of an earthly home:
help us to live as the holy family,
united in love and obedience,
and bring us at last to our home in heaven;
through Jesus Christ our Lord.
ASB collect Christmas 2

Song suggestions
Any song from *Joseph and his Amazing Technicolor Dreamcoat*
Bind us together Lord (JP17, SOF11)
He's got the whole wide world (CP19, JP78)
In our work and in our play (JP108)
Shalom, my friend (JP217)
Joseph was sold as a slave (JP413)
Sometimes I'm naughty (JP460)
Lord of the home (AMNS494)
O God in heaven (AMNS407)

The Passover
Exodus 12

Themes

God's sovereignty

God's people seemed powerless against the powerful Pharaoh and the people of Egypt. But it is God who has real power: the evil Pharaoh cannot stop God's plans for his chosen people. God forces Pharaoh to 'Let my people go,' and provides the exodus (the way out) for his people.

Deliverance and freedom

God's people are delivered from their enemies and are freed. They are free from slavery and free to worship God. The story shows how good and God's plans will triumph, so that people can be really free to follow Him.

For Jews, the eight-day festival of Pesach, or Passover, is a festival to remember how God intervened decisively in their history. The freedom gained from Pharaoh at the first Passover is symbolic of the freedom from oppression experienced throughout history.

Jesus' last meal with his disciples before his crucifixion was probably a Passover meal. At this meal Jesus said that the bread was his body and the wine was his blood. After Easter his friends understood that he was telling them that his death and his rising again show that God rescues his people not just from slavery in Egypt but also from their sins.

ASB links

Maundy Thursday Years One and Two and Christmas 2 Year One

Bible quotation

And you shall observe the feast of unleavened bread, for on this very day I brought your hosts out of the land of Egypt.
Exodus 12 v17, RSV

The epic story of the Passover and the exodus of the Israelites from Egypt to the Promised Land is the story of the birth of a nation. The book of Exodus tells how God commanded Moses to lead his people out of their slavery in Egypt and set them free in the Promised Land.

God 'hardens' the heart of Pharaoh, who refused Moses' request from God to 'Let my people go, that they may serve me.' Plagues were sent on the Egyptians but still Pharaoh refused to give in. Then God gave Moses precise instructions for taking his people out of Egypt. Each family had to take a lamb which was to be killed on the 14th of the month. The blood from the lamb had to be put on the doorposts of the houses where the Israelites were eating. God instructed the people to eat the lamb, unleavened bread and bitter herbs during their last night in Egypt. That night God 'passed over' the houses of the Israelites and the first born 'both man and beast' of the Egyptians were killed.

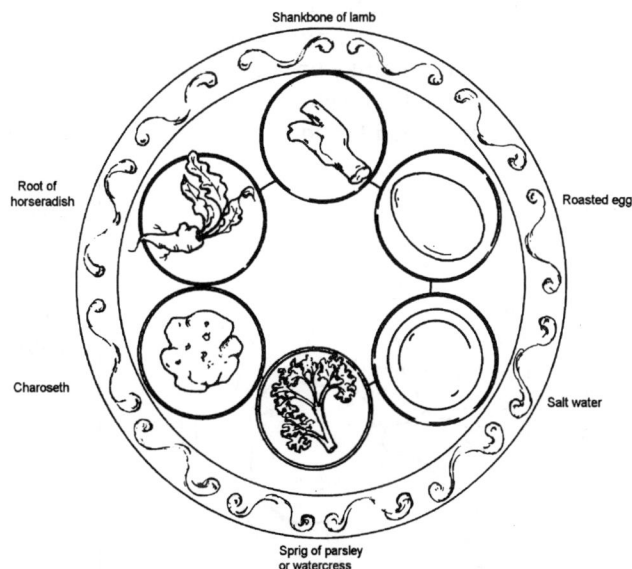

Shankbone of lamb
Root of horseradish
Roasted egg
Charoseth
Salt water
Sprig of parsley or watercress

God instructed the Israelites to keep the Passover as a memorial day. When Pharaoh saw what had happened he urged Moses and his brother Aaron to leave Egypt quickly with their people.

Introduction to the activities

Today Jewish people celebrate Passover once a year. The highlight of the festival is the opening meal, the Seder. The Seder recalls the first Passover. The various foods remind the people of the exodus and their freedom from slavery.

By making some of the foods for a Seder meal in these activities children are visually reminded of the Exodus story.

The first three Gospels link the Last Supper with a Passover meal. This theme is explored briefly in the worship suggestions and could be linked with Maundy Thursday or further work on the Eucharist.

ACTIVITIES

Rescue and escape

Younger children

The aim of these activities is to highlight the theme of deliverance.

Game

Play 'tag' games with the children. When a child is 'tagged' they have to stand still until another child touches them and releases them.

After the game retell the Exodus story of how the Israelites were slaves in Egypt and how God rescued them from their enemies. Once they had been made free they had to quickly leave Egypt and go to the Promised Land.

Activity – unleavened bread

You will need

250g plain flour
a pinch of salt
a little oil
water to bind

The Israelites had to leave Egypt so quickly that they could not make bread with yeast because there was not enough time to leave the dough to rise. So instead of ordinary bread Moses instructed them to make bread without yeast – unleavened bread. The children can make their own unleavened bread to eat during the worship.

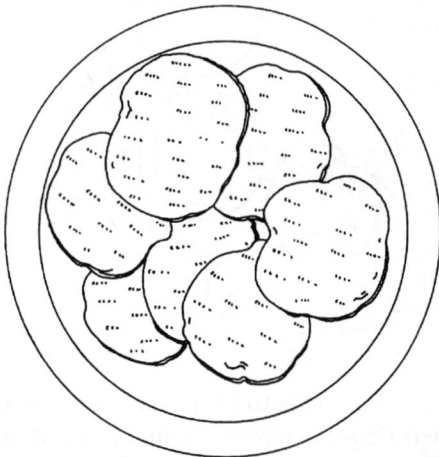

Most Jewish families in the West buy ready-prepared matzah (plural matzot), which look like large biscuit crackers. This unleavened bread is eaten during Passover as commanded in Exodus so that Jews can relive the Exodus experience.

Instructions for bread making

- Mix together the flour and the salt.

- Stir in the oil and enough water to make a stiff dough.

- Take balls of the dough and press into flat rounds and prick several times with a fork.

- An adult should then heat a griddle or non-stick frying pan and add a little oil and carefully cook the breads on both sides.

- When the breads are cool ask the children to compare them with the bread they usually eat.

Older children

Freedom from slavery

The aim of these activities is to provide visual reminders of how the Israelites received their freedom from slavery.

Game

Divide the children into groups of four. Three of the children should hold hands and then tangle themselves up not letting go of each other's hands. The fourth child has to disentangle them and set them free.

After the game retell the Exodus story about how the Israelites were in slavery. The Egyptians forced them into hard labour. They had to make bricks.

In the Seder meal Jews are reminded of this forced labour and slavery by the Charoseth. This is a paste made from fruit and nuts which is a visual reminder of the mortar used with the bricks.

Activity – making Charoseth

You will need

75g walnuts
1/4 large cooking apple
2 level teaspoons of sugar
2 level teaspoons of cinnamon
grape juice to moisten

- Mince or chop the walnuts and the apple.

- Add the sugar and cinnamon.

- Moisten with grape juice to make a stiff paste.

All age

A Passover plate

If possible invite a member of a Jewish community to come and talk with the group about celebrating Passover and the Seder meal. The group can learn about the symbolism of the different Passover foods. If possible bring examples of the foods given below. The group can then make their own Passover plates.

Background on the Seder meal

Pesach/Passover: the name Pesach comes from Exodus 12 v27 when God 'Passed over' the homes of the Jews. In Jewish homes before the Passover, all foods containing yeast/leaven must be removed from the home. Houses are spring-cleaned and special Passover dishes and cutlery taken out. Foods are prepared for the great festival. Special Passover foods are bought for the Pesach plate and these play an important part in the Seder meal, the main feast of Passover.

On the passover plate are placed:

- A roasted shankbone of lamb: this recalls the lamb that the Jews were told to sacrifice on the night before they left Egypt.

- A roasted egg: symbolic of the festival offering brought into the Temple at this season.

- A root of horseradish: to symbolise the bitter life the Jews endured in their slavery.

- A dish of salt water: thought to recall the tears the Jews endured during their slavery.

- A sprig of parsley or watercress: to symbolise the springtime of new hope when the Jews went to the Promised Land.

- Charoseth: a mixture of apples, nuts and wine, representing the mortar which held together the bricks made by the slaves.

Unleavened bread/matzot (the first unleavened bread was baked by the Jews the night they left Egypt) and wine are also set out

The festival is introduced with the Seder meal (Seder simply means order). Customs surrounding the meal vary but the heart of the ritual meal remains constant: the retelling of the story of the Israelites' oppression by Pharaoh, of the first Passover and the escape into the desert in response to four questions from the youngest family member which begin: 'Why is this night different from all other nights?'

The text for the Seder meal is called the Haggadah, or 'the telling'. It contains history, commentary, fables, legends, stories, prayers and songs.

A full description of the Seder meal can be found in books on Jewish festivals. *Judaism: An approach for GCSE* by CM Pilkington is helful.

When details of the Seder meal have been explained to the group they can make their own Passover plates by drawing the Passover foods listed above on a large paper plate as shown in the diagram.

WORSHIP

The leader can use the foods made in the activities in the worship. Explain to the children that Jesus' last meal was probably a Passover meal. When Jesus passed the unleavened bread and wine he said 'this is my body; this is my blood'. Christians remember the Last Supper at the Eucharist. Just as the Passover was the sign of the first covenant between God and humanity, the Last Supper celebrates the new relationship or second covenant between God and humankind.

Prayer

Almighty God, we thank you for bread and for all that we eat. As we remember how you brought the Israelites out of Egypt help us not to forget all those people who are still slaves or not free. Please be with us when life is difficult for us. May we trust in you like Moses did. Amen.

Song suggestions

When Israel was in Egypt's land (JP276)
Bread of heaven, on thee we feed (AMNS271, EH304)
Let us break bread together on our knees (AMNS480)
Our Father who is in heaven (JP192)
Have you got an appetite? (JP357, SOF54)
The Lord's Prayer (CP51)

Crossing the Red Sea
Exodus 13 v18-14, v30

Themes

God looks after his people

He provided directions for them through the wilderness. He gave them a pillar of cloud to follow by day and a pillar of fire to follow at night. Later on he provided his people with food and drink.

People find it hard to trust God

Despite God's intervention in Egypt, the people of Israel did not trust that God would lead them to the Promised Land. When they saw the Egyptians following them they panicked, jeered at Moses and gave up hope.

God's power

God is shown in the story to have power over nature. He caused winds and parted the sea. God also ensured that Pharoah and his subjects failed despite their superior transport. God hardened Pharoah's heart: 'I will make him stubborn, and he will pursue you, and my victory over the king and his army will bring me honour. Then the Egyptians will know that I am the Lord.'
Exodus 14 v4, GNB

ASB links

Easter day Year One and Two

Did you know?

The Red Sea is unlikely to be the Red Sea we know today. The Hebrew literally means Sea of Reeds. It is thought to be a series of lakes and marshes between the head of the Gulf of Suez and the Mediterranean. It is also used of the Gulf of Suez and the Gulf of Aqaba which are the northern arms of the Red Sea.

When the Israelites left Egypt, God led them by a pillar of cloud in the day and by a pillar of fire at night. He led them through the desert towards the Red Sea. Pharoah and his people pursued the Israelites with chariots and horses. The people were frightened and asked Moses 'Is it because there are no graves in Egypt that you have taken us away to die in the wilderness?' (Exodus 14 v11, RSV) and cried out that it would be better to work for the Egyptians than to die. Moses assured his people that God 'will work for you'.

The Israelites came to the Red Sea. Here God commanded Moses to send his people forward, lift his rod and stretch out his hand over the sea to divide it so that the people might walk across dry land. Moses did as God commanded him and the sea was drawn back and the waters divided. The people walked across. God 'hardened the hearts' of the Egyptians so that they followed the Israelites. The Egyptian chariots got bogged down in the path. God commanded Moses to stretch his hand over the sea again and the waters returned, drowning the Egyptians and swamping all their chariots. Then Miriam, the sister of Moses and Aaron, took up her tambourine, and led the people in song and dance: 'Sing to the Lord, because he has won a glorious victory; he has thrown the horses and their riders into the sea' (Exodus 15 v21, GNB).

ACTIVITIES

Parting of the sea

This activity illustrates how God looked after the Israelites by parting the waters of the Red Sea. God looked after his people through the leadership of Moses. This activity also explores the theme of leadership and care.

Before the session

- Redraw or photocopy the picture on the previous page onto A4 paper and make a copy for each child.

- Collect drawing and colouring materials.

In the session

Tell the children that there are often times when we need help. Perhaps share a personal experience with them. Ask the children what they would do or who they would turn to if they found themselves lost in a shop, or suddenly out of depth in a swimming pool, or stuck up a tree, or locked in the bathroom, or bullied at school.

Discuss how in these situations children look for a responsible adult to help. Whenever the Israelites got into trouble or had problems they turned to Moses for help, who in turn looked to God.

To make the Red Sea picture

- Give each child a copy of the picture.

- Fold along the lines shown.

- Holding the flaps down they should copy the picture below onto the back of the flaps.

- Open the flaps and colour in the picture of the Israelites actually crossing the Red Sea.

- The children can now retell the story to each other using their models.

A puppet show

The story of how God looked after his people by parting the Red Sea is very dramatic. In making their own stick puppets and making their own theatre the children can enjoy the drama themselves.

For the puppets you will need

at least six lollipop sticks
enlarged copies of the templates illustrated
cotton wool
glue and spreaders
drawing materials
scissors
card

For the scenery you will need

a sheet of yellow paper to represent the desert
a piece of blue material (a sheet, towel or curtain) to drape over a row of chairs to make the stage front and Red Sea
a strip of yellow paper or material to make the parting of the Sea

Retell the story of the crossing of the Red Sea. Then allocate the different tasks for the children to do.

- Colour the template figures (see next page).

- Stick cotton wool on the pillar of cloud.

- Stick the figures and cloud to lollipop sticks.

- Fix the yellow sheet of paper to a wall for the background scenery.

- Three feet in front of the background sheet place a row of three chairs with the seats facing outwards and cover with the blue material.

- The children can retell the story using the lollipop stick puppets behind the chairs.

- At the appropriate point in the story, the yellow strip of material can be placed along the top of the chairs to illustrate how the sea was parted and the Israelites crossed on dry land.

A book of God's powerful acts

In the story of the crossing of the Red Sea God uses his power to act decisively in Israel's history. This activity explores other Bible stories where God demonstrates his power over nature.

Before the session

Make a book for each group of children from A4 sugar paper.

You will need

A4 sheets of paper
drawing materials
glue
children's versions of the Bible stories

In the session

Retell the story of the crossing of the Red Sea. Remind the children how the Red Sea was parted. Find out if they know of any other stories in the Bible where God demonstrates his power over nature: Noah and the flood (Genesis 7 v4), during a battle Joshua asks God to stop the sun (Joshua 10 v12-14), Elijah and the ravens (1 Kings 17 v4), the story of Jonah – God sends a storm (Jonah 1 v4), a big fish (Jonah 1 v17), the Easter story (Mark 16 v6).

- Divide the children into groups of mixed ages with at least one good reader in each group.

- Ask the reader to read one of the above stories to the group (including the story of crossing of the Red Sea).

- Ask the children to draw a sequence of pictures on A4 paper, which tells the story of God's power over nature in the story they have read.

- Ask the children to write a caption for each picture on the page.

- Give each group a sugar paper book to stick their pictures into.

- Read the finished stories to all the children and ask them to suggest a title for each book.

WORSHIP

Theme: Thanking God for those who help and guide children

The worship could include the puppet show.

Prayer

Father God, we thank you for those who love and care for us each day; especially our teachers, parents and family. We thank you that they like Moses guide us safely through difficult situations. We ask that you will be a guide for all of us in all we do this week. Amen.

Song suggestions

How did Moses cross the Red Sea (JP83)
Father, lead me day by day (JP43)
God is our guide (JP56)
One more step along the world I go (JP188)
Your hand, O God has guided (JP298)
God has promised (CP31)
O worship the king (AMNS101, EH466)
Father, Lord of all creation (AMNS356)
Come, ye faithful, raise the strain (AMNS76, EH131)

Moses

Pharoah

Egyptian in chariot

Group of Israelites and animals

Pillar of cloud

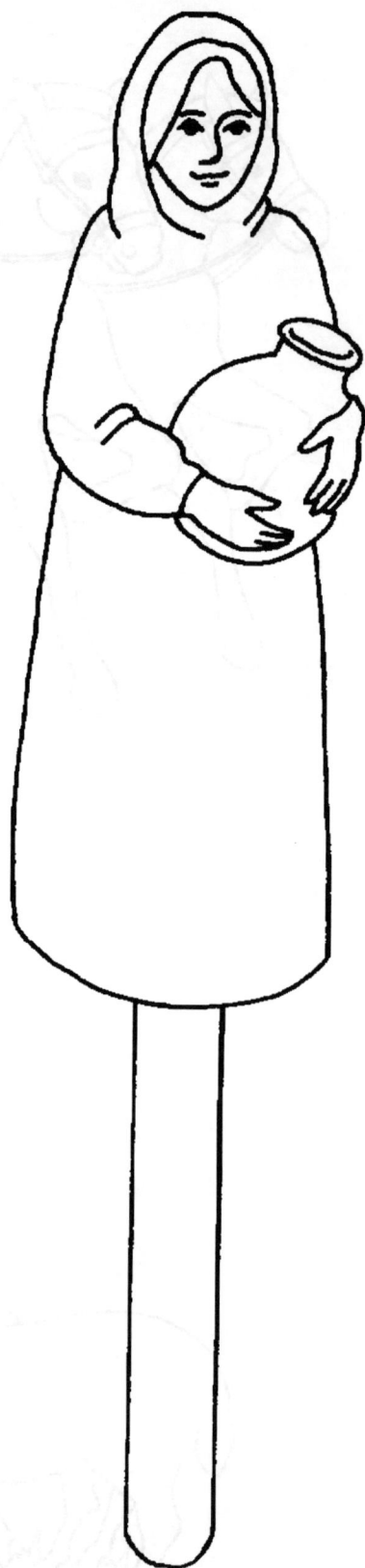

Model on
stick

Miriam

The Ten Commandments

Exodus 20

Themes

Love God

The ten commandments set out basic rules for living. The first four commandments set out a guide for a good relationship with God. They acknowledge and observe God's identity, his nature and name, his day and his claims on people.

Love your neighbour

The next six commandments give absolute laws which lay down the fundamental and essential moral requirements for a community to live in harmony. These laws are prohibitions. Any violation of these laws is a violation to the whole community.

ASB link

Pentecost 5 Year One

After their escape from slavery in Egypt, the Israelites were led by God through the desert to Mount Sinai. Here God appeared to Moses and gave him the ten commandments, the laws his people were to obey. The ten commandments cover rules for the fundamentals of community life.

Jesus gave two commandments which summarised these: 'You shall love the Lord your God with all your heart, and with all your soul, and with all your mind. This is the great and first commandment. And a second is like it, you shall love your neighbour as yourself.' (Matthew 22 v37-39, RSV).

ACTIVITIES

Discussion

It is important for the leader to explain in their own words what the ten commandments say. One way of doing this is to rewrite them in words that children understand.

1 Worship God alone.

2 God is greater than anything people can make, do or invent.

3 God's name is special and should not be misused.

4 Sunday is a holy day. It is important that people have a day of rest when they can think especially about God.

5 Be loving in thought and action to your mum, dad or those who look after you.

6 Do not murder.

7 Be faithful to your husband or wife.

8 Do not steal – it is wrong to take something which belongs to someone else.

9 Always tell the truth about other people. Telling stories about others is wrong.

10 Be content with what you have – the family you belong to, the toys you have – God will provide your needs.

Write the commandments (see ASB p161-164) on two separate cards and hide them in the room. Tell the children how God rescued the Israelites from Egypt and how they came to Mount Sinai. Explain that God told Moses to come up the mountain and there Moses received the ten commandments inscribed on two blocks of stone. Ask one of the children to find the two cards and bring them back to the group. Explain that God's rules are not only important to the Israelites but important to us today. Read out the first four commandments and say how they set out our duty towards God and then read out the last six and explain how they set out ways we relate to other people.

A patchwork of love

Younger children

This activity illustrates how God's love is like that of a very special parent.

You will need

sheets of A4 paper
a large sheet of paper
drawing materials
a large sheet of card
scissors
glue
spreaders

Discussion

Ask the children to write a list of all the things they are not allowed to do. When complete go through the list and ask them why they are not allowed to do certain things. Explain that some things are forbidden because their parents do not want them to come to any harm. Children understand this and know that their parents love them, and so usually do as they are told.

God gave Moses ten commandments or rules which the Israelites had to obey. Jesus summarised these by saying that we must love God first and love each other. Explain that God is like a very special parent who loves us so much that he gives us rules to help us live in harmony with one another.

Activity

Ask the children

- How can they show their love to their family and friends?

- What can they do?

- How can they show their love to God, e.g. by finding out more about him, by coming to church, talking to him (praying) and by reading about him in the Bible?

Hand out a sheet of A4 paper to each child and ask them to draw either a picture of themselves showing love and care for each other or love for God.

When they have finished the pictures these can be mounted on a large sheet of paper. On the border of this paper can be written the commandments Jesus gave.

Older children

Following the Maker's instructions

These activities illustrate how rules and laws are essential for living.

You will need

a variety of games: a board game, a construction kit, a lego kit, tangrams, colouring by numbers, wordsearch
clay
rolling pins
table coverings
tools for writing in the clay
paint or clay glaze

God gave his people rules to live by. Most children are familiar with the rules for games. Without rules the games become meaningless. God's laws ensured that people lived in harmony with each other and with God. Encourage the children to play the games you have brought in without giving them any instructions or rules.

Before they get too frustrated hand out the instructions and help the children complete their tasks. Ask them

- How well did they manage without the instructions?

- What difference did the instructions make?

Clay commandments

Give each child a block of clay. Ask them to

- Carefully roll out the clay to make two tiles.

- Decorate the edges of these two tiles on the borders.

- Write the words 'Love God' on one tile and on the other 'Love each other' with a blunt pencil or clay instrument.

- Dry out the tiles during the following week.

- Glaze or paint the tiles once they are dry.

Making a banner

All age

These banners provide Jesus' summary of the ten commandments. See if there is a place in your church where the ten commandments are written down. These banners can be displayed in church or used in a worship service.

You will need

long sheets of wallpaper or material
drawing materials
collage materials
glue
spreaders
scissors
templates for letters
garden canes
string

Before the session

- Make two banners out of material or wallpaper.

- Prepare letter templates for two banners. 'Love God' and 'Love each other'.

In the session

- Hand out a letter template to each child and ask them to fill it in with colour or collage materials.

- Stick the completed letters on the two banners to make the two commandments.

- If there is time ask the group to draw pictures of themselves underneath the lettering showing their love of God or love of their neighbour.

- Use garden canes and string to hang the banners up.

WORSHIP
Theme: Love God. Love your neighbour.

Use the clay commandments, patchwork and banners as a focus for worship.

Prayer

Encourage the children to stand in a circle and hold hands.

Lord, you are the God of love. Help us to love our families and our friends and show your love in all we do and say. Amen.

Song suggestions

A new commandment (JP303, SOF5)
God is love (CP36)
I lift my hands (SOF83)
Help us, O Lord, to learn (AMNS373)

Balaam and his donkey
Numbers 22

Themes
Blessing and cursing
In this story Balaam's curse or blessing is seen to have more importance than any military power.

In the Old Testament the Hebrew word for blessing is 'barak'. Blessing means the effective pronouncement of divine goodwill or grace. So God blesses people, he endows them or gives them his gifts. Good fortune is seen as a sign of God's blessing. Even when a blessing is pronounced by men, as in the case of Balaam's blessing, it is understood that a divine blessing is given because the person stands near to God. The older translations of the Bible also use the word 'blessing' as a translation of 'barak' when people bless God or 'speak well' of him. See Psalms 103, 104, and 145. More recent translations often translate the word as 'praise'.

God's power extends over all his creation
Although Balaam is not an Israelite God still has power over him. Balaam is called upon to curse the Israelite people but nothing can stop God fulfilling his promise to his people. He even uses animals to fulfil his purpose.

Quotation
The Lord bless you
and watch over you,
the Lord make his face
shine upon you
and be gracious to you,
the Lord look kindly on you
and give you peace;
and the blessing of God almighty,
the Father, the Son,
and the Holy Spirit,
be among you and remain with you
always. Amen.
ASB p107

When the people of Israel came to the Promised Land they came to the land of the Moabites. The King of Moab, Balak, was fearful of the Israelites and sent his messengers to Balaam, a man of magic, to come and curse the Israelites so that he could have victory over them.

God told Balaam not to go with the King's messengers and curse the Israelites because his people are 'blessed'. So Balaam sent the King's messengers back. The King then sent his princes with offers of great rewards if Balaam came. God then told Balaam to return with the messengers but to do exactly as he commanded. Next morning Balaam saddled his donkey and went with the princes. But God was angry that he went. An angel of the Lord with a sword in his hand barred the way of Balaam and his servants. Though Balaam could not see the angel, the donkey could and it turned away from the road. Balaam hit the donkey. Then they came to a narrow path between vineyards with a wall on either side. The angel stood in the narrow path and the donkey pushed against the wall and pressed Balaam's foot against the wall. Balaam again hit the donkey. The angel appeared again on a narrow path and this time the donkey lay down under Balaam. Balaam was very angry and struck the donkey. Then God gave the donkey speech and the donkey asked Balaam 'What have I done to you that you have struck me these three times?' (Numbers 22 v28, RSV). Balaam replied that the donkey had made a fool of him. The donkey reminded Balaam that he had served him so many years and had never behaved in this way before. Then the Lord 'opened the eyes' of Balaam and he saw the angel. The angel told him that he had stood in his way because Balaam was disobeying God. The angel pointed out were it not for the donkey then Balaam would have been killed. Balaam repented and offered to return home. The angel told him to go with the King's men but to speak only as God commanded him.

When he reached King Balak Balaam was taken to the mountains. God told Balaam to bless the Israelites. Balaam looked over the tribes of Israel and blessed them. This made King Balak very angry because Balaam blessed his enemies rather than cursed them.

ACTIVITIES

Younger children

A concertina book
In making a concertina book the children will discover that blessings are a two-way process between people and God. God blesses his people by giving freely. His people in turn bless God by praising and obeying him.

You will need
A4 sheets of paper folded in half lengthwise and then make three concertina folds as shown on the next page
drawing materials

Before the session

Print on one side of the book 'The Lord bless you and watch over you' and on the other side 'Bless the Lord all created things'.

The song of creation

The Benedicite can be found in the ASB on page 90 or the modern version on page 53.

Discuss this canticle of praise with the group. Read out the verses which show how all creation blesses God. Read some of the relevant verses which mention animals and people blessing God with the group.

In the story Balaam's donkey, although he was disobedient to his human master, did the right thing by not opposing the angel of God. The donkey, which is often believed to be a stupid animal, could not bless God in words but honoured him by being obedient. God blessed the donkey by giving him the gift of speech.

Go on to discuss blessings with the children. There are two blessings written down on page 107 of the ASB which might provide a useful starting point. The children may be able to recall times when they ask for God's blessing: at night they may ask God to bless them and their families and to watch over them; at meal times they may say a grace which says 'Lord bless this food to our use and ourselves to your service'. They may as a family ask for God's protection and blessing upon their home.

In the story, Balaam eventually sees the angel of God and responds by carrying out God's will and blessing God's people the Israelites. These points can be illustrated by making concertina books.

Making the concertina books

- On the side which has printed 'Bless the Lord all created things' from the Benedicite, ask the children to draw and colour in each space pictures of themselves, family and pets blessing God.

- On the other side of the concertina under the text 'The Lord bless you and watch over you' ask the children to draw and colour in each space pictures of things which we ask God's blessing for.

A dramatic reading

Older children

In reading the story in a dramatic way the story will come alive for the children.

You will need

at least six scripts for three narrators and three characters

Before the session either type out a copy of the Bible story from Numbers 22 v21-35, or alternatively you could use the version of the story in *The Dramatised Bible* (Marshall Pickering/Bible Society).

If you are using your own version separate out the different parts so that these can be marked with highlighter pen later.

Divide the passage up so that there are three narrators; one to read what God and the angel do, one to read what Balaam does and one to say what the donkey does. The spoken pieces can be read by three characters: the angel, Balaam and the donkey. Photocopy enough copies of your script for each child in your group.

Discussion

Before reading the script through with the whole group explain the background to the passage from the introduction. Bring out the

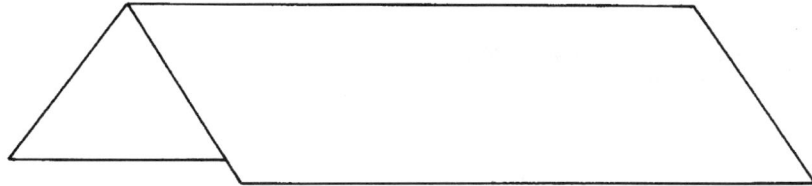

humour of the situation. God turns events upside down. Donkeys which are usually thought to be stupid animals see angels and understand; the donkey lies down and will not move; Balaam, an important man, does not understand; the donkey talks; Balaam does the opposite of what the King asks and blesses the people.

After reading the script through ask the children what they think the different characters felt like.

Dramatic reading

Divide the children up to read the parts. If you have more than six children the narration could be read chorally and three children could mime the actions of the main characters.

- Ask the children to read it through straight and praise any expression that they use.

- Then read it through in an overdramatised way with plenty of arm waving, tears, shouting and fear.

- Finally read it clearly with expression and dramatic pauses.

All age

Puppet making

The drama of this story can also be brought alive with these puppets which include a talking donkey.

To make the angel and Balaam you will need

empty fruit-corner yogurt pots
felt-tip pens
material pieces which go round the
*   circumference of the pot and over an arm*
wool for hair
PVA glue
spreaders
scissors

Making the angel and Balaam

- Turn the yogurt pot upside down. The smaller section is the bottom of the face and the large section the top of the head. The joint in the middle acts like a hinge and opens and shuts like a mouth.

- Over the hinge draw the mouth with felt-tip pens. Draw in the eyes on the top half.

- Stick wool for hair on the top surface.

- Stick material on the outside edge of the pot.

- The children put their hands into the pot with the thumb at the bottom and fingers on the top of the hinge and make the mouth speak. The material should cover the top half of their arm.

To make the donkey you will need

a cereal packet
brown paper
string
paper fasteners
scissors
string
reinforcing rings
drawing materials
extra card

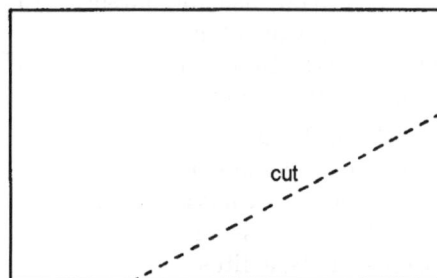

Making the donkey

1 Cover the cereal box in brown paper. Cut the box as shown above.

2 On the shorter side of the smaller section pierce a small hole as shown and thread a piece of string through the hole. Secure the hole with a reinforcing ring. Thread string through the hole and over the top of the

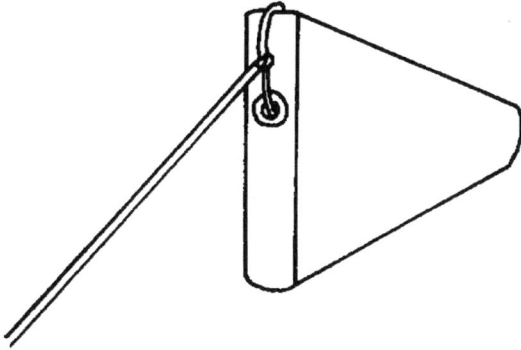

model as shown and knot.

3 On the larger box section pierce a small hole half way along the shorter side and use a reinforcing ring to strengthen the hole. Thread the string from the smaller section through this back hole.

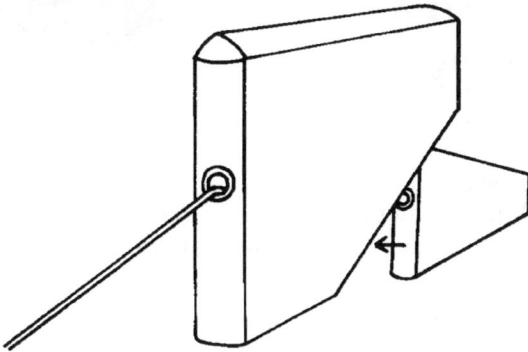

4 Slot the smaller part of the box inside the larger section. Carefully push a sharp point through at point A and secure the smaller box with paper fasteners as shown. Repeat on the other side of the model.

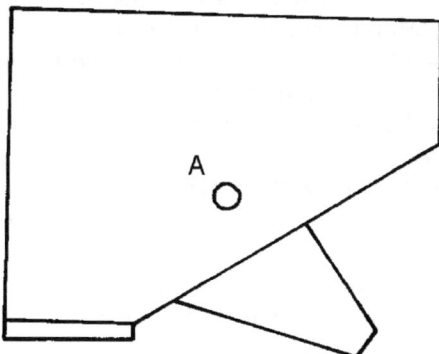

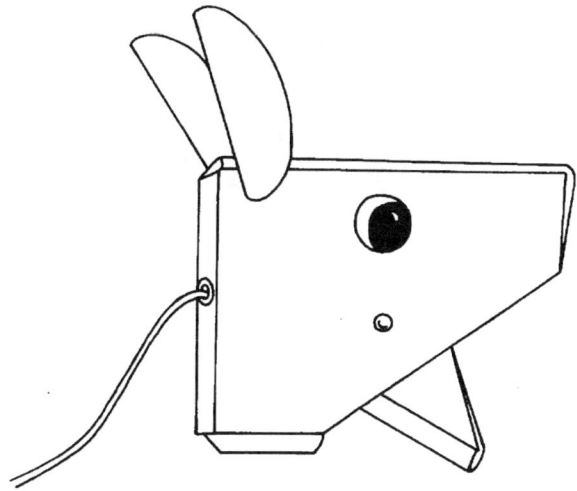

5 Make card ears and add them to the model. Draw in the eyes.

6 By pulling the string the children will be able to move their models and make the donkey talk.

Divide the children into groups of three with a donkey, Balaam and an angel and ask the children to retell the story using the puppets.

WORSHIP
Theme: Asking for God's blessing

Prayer
Adapt the blessing given as the quotation at the beginning of this chapter.

Song suggestions
Oh! Oh! Oh! how good is the Lord (JP180)
Lord dismiss us with your blessing (JP155)
Now thank we all our God
(AMNS205, EH533, JP175, CP38)
Praise God from whom all blessings flow
(JP199, SOF150)
Bless the Lord, O my soul (JP19)
Praise the Lord! ye heavens, adore him
(AMNS195, CP35, EH535)
Praise, my soul, the king of heaven
(AMNS192, EH470, JP204)

Joshua and the battle of Jericho
Joshua 6

Themes

God keeps his promises
The writers of the book of Joshua believed that God intervened decisively in the Israelites' history.
He led them to the Promised Land and then ensured that the Israelites won the great cities of Canaan including Jericho.

God looks after faithful leaders
Joshua is the great leader and successful warrior. The writers of his story believed that his success was given by God because Joshua followed God's commandments: 'Only be strong and very courageous, being careful to do according to all the law which Moses my servant commanded you; turn not from it to the right hand or to the left, that you may have good success wherever you go.' (Joshua 1 v7, RSV)

God's protection
God's protection and presence is symbolised by the Ark of the Covenant which was carried before the people in battle.

ASB links
Pentecost 9 Year One introduces Joshua

Bible quotation
And the Lord said to Joshua, 'See, I have given into your hand Jericho, with its king and mighty men of valour. You shall march around the city, all the men of war going around the city once. Thus shall you do for six days. And seven priests shall bear seven trumpets of rams' horns before the ark; and on the seventh day you shall march around the city seven times, the priests blowing the trumpets. And when they make a long blast with the ram's horn, as soon as you hear the sound of the trumpet, then all the people shall shout with a great shout; and the wall of the city will fall down flat.'
Joshua 6 v2-5, RSV

Joshua succeeded Moses as leader of the Israelites. He led his people into the Promised Land, crossing the River Jordan to enter Canaan. The book of Joshua records the conquest of Canaan by the Israelites and shows how the land was divided between the family clans of Israel in about 1230BC.

Joshua is the great hero of these conquests. With God's guidance he captures the famous and powerful city of Jericho. The writers of the book of Joshua believe that Joshua was successful in battle because he was obedient to God.

ACTIVITIES

Younger children

Ring song
This game explores the theme of Joshua's faithful leadership.

Story game
After telling the story teach the children this song. It is sung to the tune of 'There was a princess long ago'.

The Battle of Jericho
There was a leader long ago, long ago, long ago,
There was a leader long ago, long ago.
(Action: 'Joshua' stands in the centre of a ring of children).
He led the people to Jericho, etc.
(Joshua chooses four children to go outside the ring with him).
Jericho had a big high wall, etc.
(The children in the ring hold hands and raise them high).
Then God said, 'March around the town', etc.
(One child chosen to be God cups hands round mouth).
For six days they marched around, etc.
(Joshua and the four children march round the outside of the ring).
Then the priests they blew their horns, etc.
(Joshua and the four children stand still and pretend to blow horns).
On day seven they gave a loud shout, etc.
(Joshua and four children shout at the end).
Jericho's walls came crashing down, etc.
(The ring of children fall down).
So God's people took the town, etc.
(All the children skip round clapping hands).

After the song discuss with the group how Joshua and the Israelites followed what God had told them to do even though it may have sounded a strange way to capture a city. The people followed and trusted their leader.

Reminders of God's presence

Older children

The Ark of the Covenant was a reminder of God's presence and protection to the people of Israel. Christians use the symbol of the cross to remind them of God's presence with them through Jesus. These activities explore the symbolism of the Ark of the Covenant and the cross.

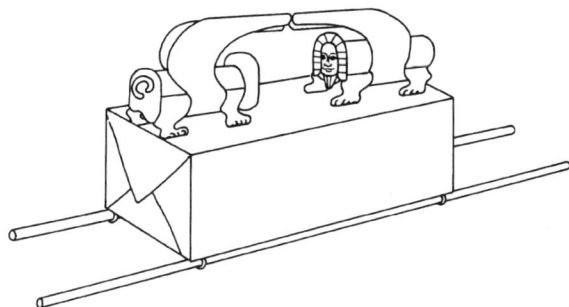

The Ark of the Covenant

The Ark was a large wooden chest which was made from acacia wood and covered with gold. It measured about four feet by two feet by two feet. (Exodus 25 v10ff). It was carried from place to place by means of long poles threaded through rings at each of the four corners of the chest. The Ark contained the two tablets of the ten commandments.

On the top of the chest (called the 'Mercy Seat') were two angelic figures called cherubim. Their wings spread across the ark and met above the Mercy Seat. The ark, the cherubim and poles were covered in gold. The Mercy Seat was seen as the place where God was enthroned 'I will meet you there, and from above the lid between the two winged creatures I will give you all my laws for the people of Israel.' (Exodus 25 v22, GNB). When Solomon built his Temple the Ark was housed in the Holy of Holies within the temple.

To make an Ark of the Covenant you will need

a shoe box approximately 21cm x 8cm x 11cm
two pea sticks
gold or yellow paper for wrapping the box
photocopies of the cherubim template
(see next page) on card
gold spray
4 small gold curtain rings
sticky tape
2 toilet roll middles
drawing materials
scissors
glue

- Cover the outside of the box with gold or yellow paper.

- Attach the curtain rings with sticky tape to the bottom of the box as shown and thread the pea sticks through.

To make one of the cherubim

- Snip 5cm at either side of each end of the cardboard rolls and fold the cardboard into the tube.

- Cut out the photocopies of the cherubim.

- Stick the underside of the cherubim around the roll and fold down the legs.

- Draw the claws on the base of the feet.

- Stick the face over the folded front end of the toilet roll.

- Stick the tail over the folded back end of the roll.

- Repeat this and make another cherub.

- When completed stick both cherubim to the top of the box, facing each other with the tips of the wings touching.

- An adult should spray the completed model with gold spray.

Cross

Explain to the children that the cross is the symbol of the Christian faith and reminds people of Jesus' death and resurrection. Just as the Ark of the Covenant reminded the Israelites of God's intervention in their history, the cross reminds Christians of God sending Jesus into the world.

Children can make their own crosses to hang in their rooms at home.

You will need

a cross shape cut from card
collage materials
masking tape
string
scissors
glue

- Cover the cross shape with collage materials.

- When completed cut a length of string and loop it round and fix onto the back of the cross with masking tape.

Recreating the battle of Jericho

All age

The battle of Jericho is such a vivid story that the children will enjoy retelling the story in drama. The drama will also remind them that God was on Joshua's side and that it was from God that Joshua received his success.

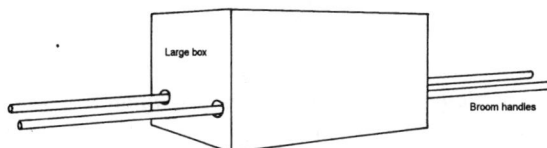

Back

Underside of Cherubim

fold

fold

Front

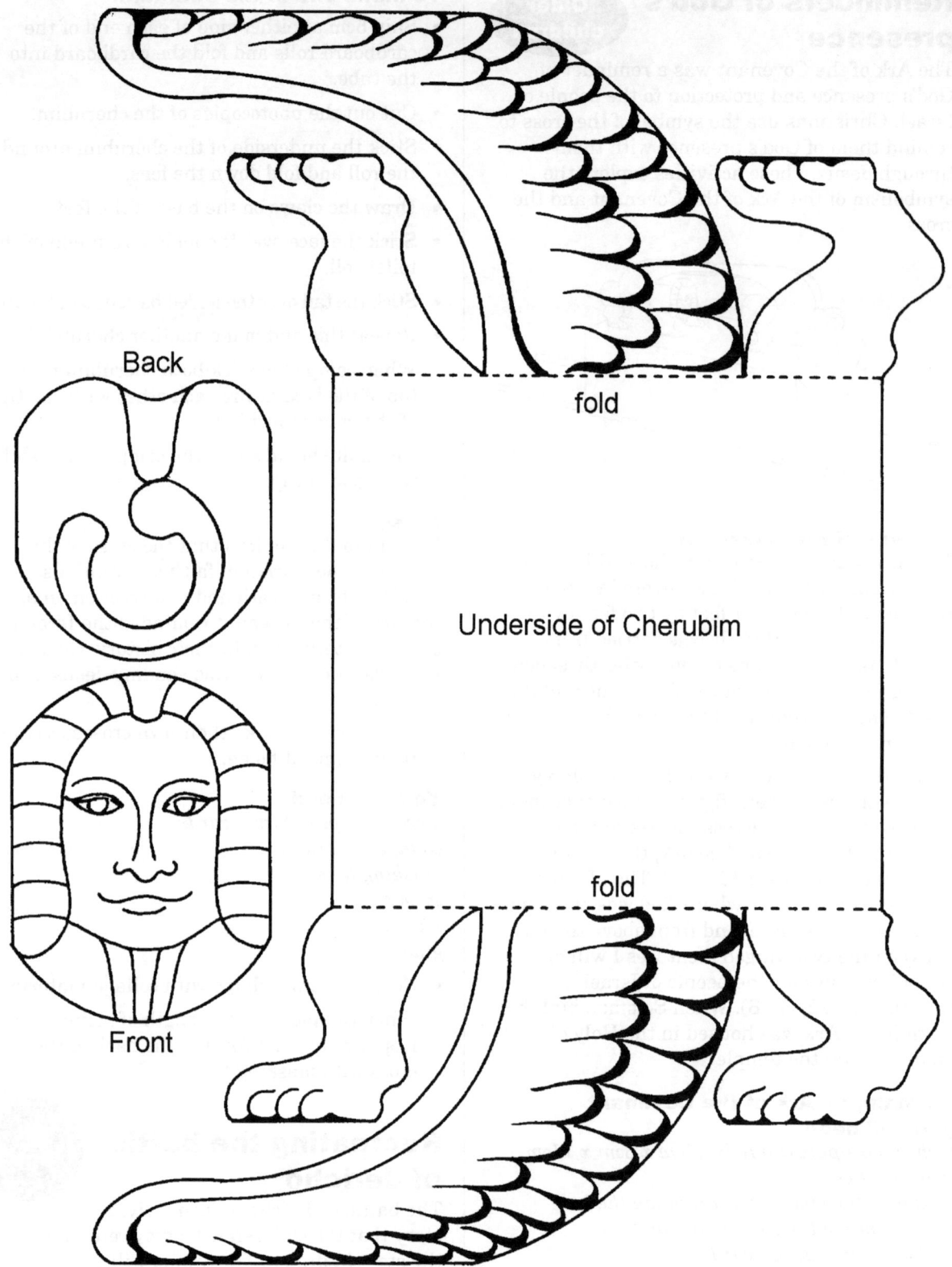

You will need these props
cardboard box
2 broom handles (thread the broom handles through the box so that it can be carried as shown on the previous page)
cardboard trumpets or real musical wind instruments (a trumpet sound can be made by blowing carefully across the open top of a large plastic bottle)
cardboard spears

Choose people to be the following characters:

the people of Israel

Joshua

a group of children for the wall

priests

the choir

If possible, learn the spiritual 'Joshua fit the battle of Jericho'. The words are given on the next page and the music is in *Junior Praise*.

This can be sung while the group enacts the drama.

Alternatively the group can act out the drama following the Biblical story.

- For the wall a group should hold up their hands in a ring to form a 'wall of Jericho'.

- Joshua leads the people of Israel around the wall. Behind Joshua walk the priests holding up the Ark. The rest of the group follows.

- When the walls come tumbling down, the wall group can all fall down.

Discussion

The people of Israel believed that the battle of Jericho was holy war they were fighting for God. Their victory was due to God. Discuss with the group:

- Is it ever right to use violence and force against your enemies?

- If someone kicks you in the playground is it right to kick them back?

- Jesus said if any one hits you on the right cheek you must turn to him the other. What do you think Jesus meant by this?

SONG: Joshua fit the battle of Jericho

Chorus
Joshua fit the battle of Jericho, Jericho, Jericho,
Joshua fit the battle of Jericho, and the walls came tumbling down.

1 You may talk about your king of Gideon,
   You may talk about your man of Saul,
   But there's none like good old Joshua
   at the battle of Jericho.

2 Up to the walls of Jericho,
   he marched with spear in hand,

'Go blow them ram-horns,' Joshua cried,
'Cause the battle am in my hand.'

3 Then the ram-sheeps' horns began to blow,
   Trumpets began to sound.
   Joshua commanded the children to shout,
   and the walls came tumbling down, that morning.

Repeat chorus

WORSHIP

Theme: Our strength is from God

Watch the all-age drama of the fall of Jericho.

- Use the cross shapes as a focus of prayer.

Prayer

Almighty God, we thank you that your son Jesus died for us, and lives with you. Defend and protect us from all dangers. Like Joshua help us to do what is right, and receive your strength and security, today and throughout the week. Amen.

Song suggestions

Joshua fit the battle of Jericho (JP143)
Now be strong and very courageous (JP172)
Be strong and courageous (SOF9)
O Jesus, I have promised (AMNS235, EH577)
God told Joshua (JP351)
We are marching (SOF176)

The strength of Samson

Judges 16

Themes

National heroes

Samson was a national folk hero. God gave the Israelites a great and strong man to succeed against their enemies despite incredible odds. Samson is shown to be wise and cunning, a lover of practical jokes but not without his weaknesses.

God chooses many different people

Samson was no saint. Yet despite his many failings God uses Samson for his purposes.

Strength comes from God

Samson's strength is a God-given gift. He loses this gift when his hair is cut. His final prayer brings back the divine aid so that by bringing the pillars down upon himself and the Philistines he kills more of the enemy in his dying than he has killed in his life.

Samson was chosen by God and dedicated from his birth to deliver his people. Samson was the son of Manoah of the tribe of Dan. His story takes place when the Philistines were a force to be reckoned with by the Israelites. Chapters 13 to 16 of the book of Judges are full of the exploits of this strong and impetuous folk hero and his conquests over the Philistines.

Although Samson was married, he went to Gaza and fell in love with Delilah. The Philistines bribed Delilah to try and trap Samson to find out the source of his strength. Three times Delilah was unsuccessful in ensnaring Samson. Finally she cajoled Samson by telling him his failure to confide in her proved his lack of love for her. After pestering him constantly Samson then told her that he was consecrated to God's service and that if his head was shaved his strength would leave him. While Samson slept Delilah ordered someone to shave Samson's head. Samson's strength left him and Delilah wakened him. The Philistines seized Samson, tortured him and put him in prison. During the time of a Philistine festival to their god Dagon, Samson was brought out of prison. The Philistines made a fool of him in front of the pillars of the building. Samson called upon God to return his strength just once. Samson leaned his arms on the two central pillars and asked the Lord 'Let me die with the Philistines'. The house fell down and many Philistines together with Samson were killed.

ACTIVITIES

Younger children

The strength of Samson

Through the telling of this exciting story the children will discover the similarity between God's man Samson, and some of their favourite cartoon heroes. Unlike cartoon heroes Samson is completely dependent on God. As a man he had many failings. His strength came from God and without God he was nothing.

I am God's Hero

Name: _____ Age: _____

Birthday: _____

Church: _____

Favourite food: _____

What I enjoy doing: _____

_____

_____

Discussion

After telling the story find out from the children the names of their favourite television and video heroes who always win despite impossible odds. If possible include women as well. Use the story of a cartoon hero from a comic to help the children discover the similarities and differences between the cartoon hero and Samson. Samson does not live happily ever after. He is not the perfect hero of children's stories today. He is far from perfect but God still chose him.

Activity 1: We are all special to God

Like Samson the children are special to God.

Hand a photocopy of the 'I am God's Hero' certificate to each child and help them fill it in and draw a picture of themselves.

Activity 2: A woven picture

To remind the group of one of the ways that Delilah tried to trap Samson by weaving his hair they can make this woven picture.

You will need

card from birthday cards or cereal boxes
scissors
wool
ribbon
paper strips for weaving
sticky tape

- Fold a piece of card into three.

- Open out the bottom third and draw the face of Samson on it.

- Cut along the lines as shown in the diagram on the remaining two-thirds of the card.

- Open the card out. Using different strips of fabric or paper weave Samson's hair as shown.

- Secure the strips on the reverse of the picture with sticky tape.

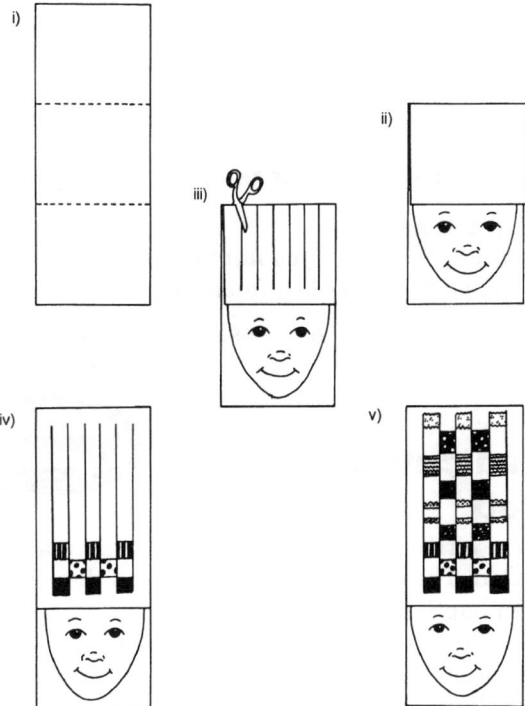

Hero posters

All age

Through the telling of the story of Samson followed by the story of a hero of the faith today the children will see that God still chooses some people to be leaders to change things for the better.

This activity would be best done over two weeks as it involves the telling of two stories.

Week 1

Tell the story of Samson choosing stories from Judges 13 to 16.

Activity: A poster of Samson

You will need

books with pictures about Samson and the Philistines and pictures which show life at the time of Samson
a poster-sized sheet of paper
individual sheets of paper
glue
drawing materials

- Divide the children up to do the different parts of the poster.
- On the large sheet draw and colour a large picture of Samson similiar to the picture at the beginning of the chapter.
- On the smaller sheets ask the children to illustrate events from Samson's life and write a sentence about the event underneath.
- Stick the pictures around the picture of Samson.
- Write a heading at the top of the poster such as 'Samson the Strong'.

Week 2

Tell the story of a modern hero of faith e.g. Archbishop Oscar Romero, Mother Teresa, Archbishop Desmond Tutu, Jackie Pullinger etc. Choose parts of their story which show their strengths and weaknesses and how their faith has led them.

Activity: A poster of the modern day hero

You will need

pictures of the 'hero' you have chosen and books about the issues they have been involved in

- Make a modern hero poster in the same way as the Samson poster.

Dedicated to follow God

Older children

From birth Samson's life had been consecrated to God. The children will learn that if they have been baptised their parents and godparents have promised to bring them up in the Christian faith. If possible take the children into church to take part in a baptism service.

Discussion

After telling the story of Samson explain that Samson's parents had set him apart for God from birth. Samson was a Nazirite (Nazirites dedicated themselves to God and promised never to cut their hair, drink wine, eat unclean food or touch a dead body).

When children are baptised today their parents and godparents promise to bring them up in the Christian faith to fight against sin and to follow Christ. The priest makes the sign of the cross on the forehead of the child and says, 'Do not be ashamed to confess the faith of Christ crucified.' And the congregation join in and say 'Fight valiantly under the banner of Christ against sin, the world, and the devil, and continue his faithful soldier and servant to the end of your life'. Samson had the gift of strength from God. At baptism we receive the gift of the Holy Spirit which gives us the strength to stand up for what is right.

Go on to discuss these questions with the group:

- What things do the children have to stand up for at school? Explain that Christians follow the example in the life of Jesus in the way they should behave towards God and towards others.
- When is it particularly difficult to do what is right?
- Are there times when it is difficult to know what is right?

Incorporate some of the points from this discussion in the worship time.

WORSHIP

Theme: Thanking God that we are members of his family and special to him

Prayer

Thank you God that we are part of your family;
we are members together of the body of Christ;
we are children of the same heavenly Father;
we are inheritors together of your kingdom.
Amen.
Adapted from the welcome at baptism, ASB p248

Song suggestions

Jesus, good above all other
(AMNS378, CP23, EH598)
Go, tell it on the mountain (CP24, JP65)
We are one, we are family (SOF175)
We are in God's army (SOF173)
Be strong and courageous (SOF9)
We've got a lot of hope (SOF181)
We are soldiers of the king (JP483)
So we're marching along (JP459, SOF160)
Eternal God, we consecrate (AMNS452)
O Jesus, I have promised (AMNS235, EH577)
Soldiers of Christ, arise (AMNS219, EH479)

Ruth the Moabitess
The book of Ruth

Themes
Ruth's loyalty
When Ruth's first husband died she had nothing. Naomi encouraged her to return to her own family but instead Ruth stayed with her mother-in-law. She travelled to a strange land and lived amongst a foreign people making sure that Naomi was provided for.

God's kingdom is for all people
The Old Testament is a history of how God's people, the Israelites, enjoyed a favoured relationship with God. Although there are many Old Testament stories about how the Israelites maintained the purity of their religion from outside contamination, the story of Ruth shows how faith in the God of Israel is open to all people, even a Moabitess, an outsider. Sometimes God chooses outsiders or unlikely people to fulfil his promises.

ASB links
Pentecost 5 Year Two

Bible quotation
For where you go I will go, and where you lodge I will lodge; your people shall be my people, and your God my God.
Ruth 1 v16, RSV

The story of Ruth in the Old Testament is unique. It is of a woman from outside Israel who through her trust and loyalty came to be the great-grandmother of David, the greatest of all the kings of Israel.

The story is set in the period of the Judges (1200-1070 BC). Elimelech and his wife Naomi and their two sons Mahlon and Chilion, left Bethlehem during a famine to go to Moab. In Moab both sons took Moabite wives. But Elimelech and his two sons died, leaving Naomi with her two daughters-in-law, Ruth and Orpah. Naomi decided to return to Judah and encouraged her daughters-in-law to return to their own homes. Ruth begged Naomi to let her stay with her and so the two women returned to Bethlehem. Ruth worked in the fields to get enough grain so that the two women could live. Here she met Boaz, a relative of Elimelech, who was impressed with her loyalty. He ensured that she was able to collect the best of the harvest. Boaz bought Elimelech's land and married Ruth. The couple bore a son called Obed the father of Jesse and grandfather of David.

ACTIVITIES

Younger children

A gallery of friends
Friendships are very important to young children. It is through their experience of friendship that a more mature relationship of loyalty to a friend develops. The story of Ruth can be used to show how loyalty keeps friends together through thick and thin. These two activities explore this theme.

The Vicar

Mary

The Choir

Mr. Lucas

Mrs. Reed

Jonathan

You will need
A4 sheets of paper
drawing materials
Blu-Tack

As soon as the children arrive ask them to draw a picture of one of their friends. Write the name of the friend on the sheet of paper and put it on the wall.

Ask the children to look at the gallery of friends. Encourage each child to talk about their friend to the rest of the group.

- Why do they like their friend?
- What is special about them?
- What makes them a good friend?
- What do they enjoy doing with their friends?

Tell the story of Ruth. Ruth was a good friend to Naomi. She left her own family and went with Naomi to a strange country to a village called Bethlehem. Tell the group how Naomi met and married Boaz and had a son called Obed, the grandfather of King David. Jesus, who came from Bethlehem, David's city, was also related to David.

A friendship prayer

You will need
pairs of figures
cut as shown
drawing
materials

Before the session write on the inside of one of the figures 'When my friend is lonely (crying, left out, hungry, excited, happy and hurt)'. On the other figure write, 'Lord, help me to . . .' and leave space so that the group can complete the prayer during the session.

Put on fold of paper

Friends are loyal when they stick up for you, when they help you when you are hurt and when they share their birthdays and food. Like Ruth, loyal friends stay through the bad times as well as the good. Tell the children that they are to imagine that they are in the playground at school when they notice that one of their friends is crying, lonely, left out, hungry, excited, happy or hurt. Show them one of the pair of figures you have made and ask them to help you complete the prayer inside.

Put the finished figures on the wall underneath the gallery of friends. You could use these friendship prayers in the worship.

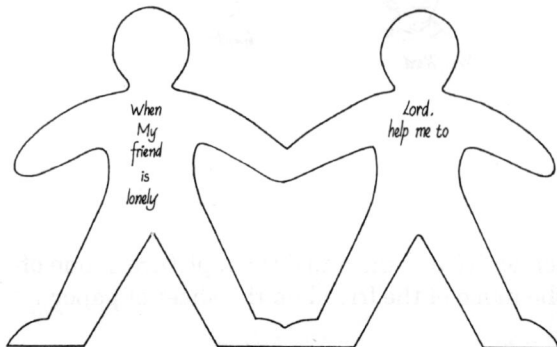

When My friend is lonely *Lord, help me to*

God's kingdom is for all people
Older children

Children often feel that because they are small and ordinary they do not count. In the story of Ruth children will find out that ordinary people like themselves are significant to God. We are all part of God's family.

You will need
an enlargement of the picture of Jesus on the previous page
small sheets of paper
drawing materials

Tell the story of how Ruth, a foreigner, came to believe in God. How she left her home country and those she knew to go to a strange land with Naomi, her mother-in-law. Ruth became accepted by Naomi's relations because of her loyalty.

We all belong to God's family whatever we look like or whoever we are. Hand out the pieces of paper and ask the children to draw or write the names of people they know who go to their own church, then the names of other people they know who go to a different church and then the names of people they know who do not go to church. Stick the completed papers around the figure of Jesus.

Then point out to the children that although people may go to different churches or no church at all, God loves all his children. Go on to discuss how they can help care for God's family just as Ruth cared for Naomi.

A 'Welcome' card
One practical way to do this is for the children to make welcome cards. Invite the children to make their own designs for a welcome card which they can give to someone new who comes to the next family service. You might like to include a leaflet which outlines the children's activities at your church.

Our own families
All age

The sense of responsibility to family and friends which both Ruth and Boaz showed is both encouraging and challenging. Many children only see their extended family on special family celebrations and may forget about their cousins, aunts and uncles unless they see them regularly. This activity helps children remember their own extended family in their prayers.

You will need
an A4 sheet of paper for each child
small pieces of paper or photographs of relations
drawing materials
scissors
glue

Discussion

Talk with the children about their larger extended family. Boaz was part of Naomi's extended family and cared for his relatives in very practical ways. Today many families experience hardship, arguments, illness, death, stress etc. Discuss how God's care for people extends through the good times and the bad. Explain the importance of prayer at these times.

A kinship collage

Obed, Ruth's son was grandfather to King David and ultimately an ancestor of Jesus. Help the children to start to put together a collage of the people in their own extended family.

- In the middle of the sheet of paper draw a picture of their immediate family.

- Around the picture stick photographs or drawings of other members of the family. These could include grandparents, uncles, aunts, cousins, brothers and sisters who have left home, and include family members who have died.

- Ask the children's parents to help the children fill it in and add extra pictures if needed. Suggest that they tell the children stories about relations they hardly know and suggest that they help the children pray for them when they go to bed.

WORSHIP
Theme: Friendship with Jesus and each other

Use the friendship prayers, the God's family picture and any finished kinship collages.

The Prayer of St Francis

Lord, make me an instrument of your peace;
Where there is hatred, let me sow love;
Where there is injury, pardon;
Where there is discord, union;
Where there is doubt, faith;
Where there is despair, hope;
Where there is darkness, light;
Where there is sadness, joy.

Song suggestions

Make me a channel of your peace (JP161, SOF135)
Jesus is a friend of mine (JP136)
Kum ba yah (CP68, JPI49)
What a friend we have in Jesus (JP273)
Oh! Oh! Oh! how good is the Lord (JP180)
When I'm feeling lonely (JP493)
When the dark clouds (JP494)
We are one, we are family (SOF175)
God loves you (SOF48, JP348)
O God in heaven, whose loving plan (AMNS407)
In Christ there is no east or west (AMNS376)
God is here; as we his people (AMNS464)

Granny and Grandpa | Uncle John. Auntie Ann and family | Uncle Jack

Uncle Andrew and Auntie Sue | Mum. Dad. Helen. Benjamin and Me | Cousin Mary and family in Australia

Auntie Sarah | Grandma and Grandad | Great Grandma Olive

The call of Samuel
1 Samuel 3

Themes

Hearing God's call

Samuel did not immediately recognise that it was God who was calling him. God's call is not necessarily always immediately obvious to people.

God does not always choose the most likely 'godly' people

At the time of Eli prophets were rare and visionaries few because the people had fallen away from God. The story of Samuel shows how God bypassed the established priesthood, the most likely 'godly' people and communicated his message to a novice, a young boy.

Prophecy

Samuel was given a prophecy by God. Like many prophets his message was not a happy one. Prophets today are not always well received.

ASB links

Epiphany 2 Year Two

Bible quotation

And Samuel said, 'Speak, for thy servant hears.'
1 Samuel 3 v10, RSV

Samuel was the son of Elkanah and Hannah. The childless Hannah had promised that if God gave her a son she would dedicate him to God. When Samuel was old enough he was taken to the priest Eli. Samuel was brought up by Eli and served God in the temple. Eli was old and nearly blind. One night both Eli and Samuel lay down in the temple where the Ark was kept. God called 'Samuel, Samuel,' and Samuel responded 'Here I am' and ran to Eli thinking that the old man had called him. Eli told him that he had not called him and told him to return to sleep. Again Samuel heard the voice and again he ran to Eli. The same thing happened. The third time he arose and went to Eli, Eli realised that it was God who was calling Samuel. Eli told Samuel that if he heard the voice again he should say 'Speak Lord, for thy servant hears.' (1 Samuel 3 v10, RSV)

Again God called Samuel and Samuel responded as Eli had instructed. God told Samuel that he was about to do something in Israel that would make the ears of everyone who heard tingle. He told him that he was going to punish Eli's family because of Eli's sons' sinfulness.

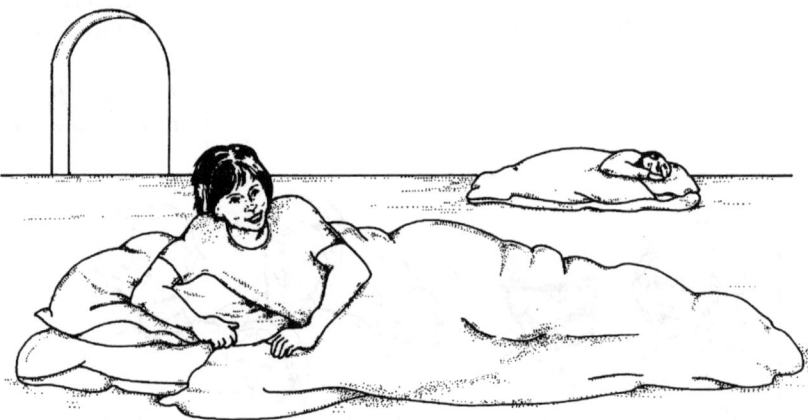

The next morning Samuel was afraid to tell Eli about what God had said but Eli insisted. Samuel grew up and he became recognised as a prophet of God.

ACTIVITIES

Younger children

Finding our vocation

Samuel heard God's call when he was a child but it was not until he had grown up that he took over from Eli. Paul likewise wrote: 'God, who set me apart from birth and called me through his grace . . .' (Galatians 1 v15, NEB from the New Testament reading for Epiphany 2 Year 2). God has a 'special job' for everyone to do.

Through this activity children think about how they too will have a 'special job' to do for God one day.

You will need

a sheet of A4 paper folded in half for each child
drawing materials

Tell the story of Samuel and emphasise that God never asks anyone to do anything they cannot do. Explain that when Samuel

I am the oldest. I have younger sisters.
I go to school.
I go to family service on Sunday.

I will be a mummy.
I want to sail around the world.
I want to be on television.
I want to hand hymn books to people in Church.

grew up he became a judge and a prophet. Ask the children what they would like to be when they grow up.

Often people have a number of jobs or roles at once. A father might be a engineer, a church organist and a football coach. A mother might be a teacher, dancer and lay reader. When Christians grow up they try to find out what it is God wants them to do with their life.

A 'growing-up' picture

- Hand out the folded sheet of paper and ask the children to draw a picture of themselves as they are now on one side.

- On the other side they should draw a picture of the adult they would like to be.

- Help them to write underneath who they are now and what they would like to be when they grow up.

- Point out to them that they may always be a brother, football supporter, reader of books and God's friend but other roles will change.

Hearing God's call

Older children

Through the telling of Bible stories which show how God has spoken to different people the children will begin to understand about the different ways God speaks to people. If possible share with the children any personal experience you have had of hearing God's 'voice'.

Story and discussion

Tell simply each of the stories below. Ask the children how the people in the story recognised God or Jesus? How did they feel about what he had told them and what was their response?

- The call of Samuel (1 Samuel 3).

- The road to Emmaus (Luke 24 v13-35).

- St Paul on the road to Damascus (Acts 9 v1-22).

Discussion and drama: What might have happened if . . . ?

Samuel had special qualities and gifts which helped him to hear what God wanted him to do. He was ready to serve God in the temple, he was willing to obey and he did not hide from the truth. The story of Samuel might have been very different if Samuel had not had these qualities.

Discuss with the children what would have happened if

- Samuel had not wanted to get out of his warm bed and go over to Eli in the dark.

- Samuel thought that old Eli was 'potty' and that God just does not speak to people and especially children.

- Samuel decided not to tell Eli the whole of what God had told him.

If there is time suggest the children divide into threes and act out the various scenarios outlined above. Then act out what really happened.

Learning to listen to God

All age

Just as it is possible to learn to pray, so it is possible to practise listening to God. After playing a listening game and discussing the importance of listening the children can be led into a short meditation.

For the games you will need
a ball

For the meditation you will need
a tape player
a tape of classical or religious music
a candle
candle holder
matches
Psalm 139 and a song to sing or the Lord's
Prayer to say at the end

Listening games
Choose a selection of games suitable for the age of children in your group. Chinese whispers is a game where listening and passing on the message are significant skills.

Ball game
Stand in a circle with one child holding the ball. A child throws the ball to someone in the group shouting out their name. Then that child throws the ball to someone else. In this game it is important to be ready, to listen for the name and to pass the ball on.

Clapping game
Sit in a circle and give each child a number. Start by clapping twice and saying your number then clap twice again and say another number in the circle. The new person then claps twice, says their number, claps twice and brings in someone else. For older children it is important to get the rhythm going. Again listening and passing the clapping on is important to the game.

Shipwreck
Different areas of the room are labelled parts of the ship (deck, cabin, engine room, galley etc.). The caller shouts out 'All on deck' and all the children go to that area. This game can be made more interesting by issuing actions such as, 'Climb the rigging' (climbing action standing on the spot), 'Man the lifeboats' (sit on the floor and row). The game involves listening and obeying the instructions given.

Discussion
Ask the children what were the important things to do when playing the game.

- **Listening**: the game depends on listening carefully. So it is with listening to God.

- **Readiness**: the game depends on taking part and being ready to go into action. So must we be ready to listen to God.

- **Obeying:** the game depends on immediate obedience to commands given. We have to obey God's commandments.

Many people find it easier to talk to God than to listen. Tell the story of Samuel. Point out to the group the following:

- God spoke when all was still.

- Samuel had to recognise God's voice and know what to do.

- Samuel was ready to go three times to Eli.

- Samuel listened to God.

- Samuel passed on God's message.

- God did not ask Samuel to do something he could not do.

Meditational prayer
Explain to the children that one way of listening to God is through meditational prayer. Make sure they are all sitting comfortably in a place where they can see what you are doing and can see the candle. Ask the children to be silent and still. Slowly get up to light the candle and put on the music. As you create the atmosphere explain to the children what you are doing.

- I am putting on quiet music to help us to be peaceful inside.

- I am lighting a candle to remind us of God's presence with us here, of his warmth and love for us and of the light that he gives us to show us his way.

- I am going to read part of Psalm 139 and you can close your eyes and make pictures in your mind of what I am reading. Let your thoughts wander when I stop reading. Or open your eyes and think about what I am reading while looking at the burning candle.

- I am going to pray and ask God to speak of his love for each one of us in our hearts.

Loving Father, we thank you that you knew us before we were born, that you love each one of us. Help us to feel your love in our hearts, now and always. Amen

After another time of quiet finish by all saying the Lord's Prayer or a favourite song or hymn they all know.

If you do not get past the lighting of the candle before the atmosphere is broken, say the prayer and suggest that they all join in singing a song. Try and do a bit more next week. Children may laugh because they are embarrassed, because they have never done anything like this before or because the idea that God might speak to them is frightening. Take time to reassure them that God never asks anyone to do something they cannot do.

Allow a time at the end for the children to talk about what they have experienced. Often in sharing our experiences, others who have not felt anything in particular are encouraged.

WORSHIP
Theme: Thanking God for loving us and asking him to help us to listen to him

Prayer
Use the meditational prayer.

Song suggestions
Be still and know that I am God (JP22)
Let God speak (SOF120)
I listen and I listen (CP60)
Jesus calls us (AMNS312, EH205)
Lord Jesus, once you spoke to men (AMNS392)
Rise and hear! The Lord is speaking (AMNS509)

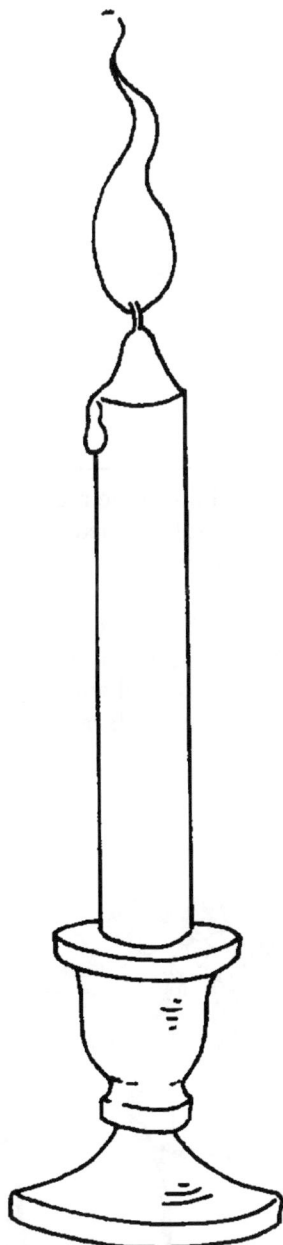

King Saul
1 Samuel 8-10

Themes
Kingship
The Israelites wanted to be like other nations and have a king to rule over them. God finally agreed to provide his people with an earthly king. Saul's consecration is shown through the anointing with oil.

Anointing
In the story, Samuel pours oil on Saul's head and Saul is anointed by God. Saul is set apart, consecrated, by this anointing to be king over his people on God's behalf. In the Old Testament anointing is given to kings, priests and prophets. It marks a setting apart by God for a special purpose. Kings received God's power to rule over Israel and this divine selection as well as the reception of authority is part of the story of Saul's anointing.

In the New Testament Jesus is the 'Christ', which like Messiah means the Anointed One. His kingship is shown to be very different from that expected by his followers. In Christian times anointing became a sacrament of physical healing and spiritual strengthening. An anointing with oil signified the reception of the Holy Spirit. Today the king or queen of England is still anointed with oil. Anointing of a Christian happens at baptism, confirmation, ordination and consecration. Holy oil can also be used to anoint very sick or dying people.

ASB links
The story of the anointing of Saul is not in the ASB Sunday lectionary. The activities suggested here can be used for Epiphany 1 Year One for the story of the anointing of David (1 Samuel 16 v1-13).

When Samuel was an old man the elders of Israel came to him and asked for a king to govern them. Samuel was displeased at their request and prayed to God. God affirmed that he was the king of his people and that Samuel should warn his people about the demands an earthly king would make upon them. Samuel went and warned the Israelites that a king would make demands on their goods, their relations and their wealth but the people refused to listen to him and continued to demand a king so he could govern them and lead them into battle. Samuel again spoke with God and God told him to give his people a king.

A handsome man of the tribe of Benjamin whose name was Saul was searching for his father's asses in the area where Samuel was. Saul's servant suggested that they ask Samuel for help. Samuel had been instructed by God to anoint Saul to be ruler over the Israelites. When Samuel met Saul he gave Saul a special meal. The next morning Samuel anointed Saul with oil and told him that God had made him king over all Israel.

ACTIVITIES
King making

This activity makes a link between King Saul and the present Queen and illustrates that both are God's servants and have a responsibility to work for the good of their people.

You will need

a crown (from a cracker or a nativity play)
a series of commands written on slips of paper and put in a bowl
materials that are needed to carry out the commands
a tape recorder
a cassette of regal music

The series of commands should ask children to do things that servants do for others, e.g. wash children's hands; hand out sweets, biscuits or drinks for the children; find out who has been ill recently, lost a football match, broken a favourite toy etc and show concern; tell a joke, sing a song or do a dance to entertain their friends and so on.

Discussion

Show the two pictures illustrated of Elizabeth II and Saul being made sovereigns. Can they describe what is happening? Where is it happening? What are the similarities and what are the differences?

Tell the story of Saul explaining that the people of Israel had no king and were being attacked by their enemies. God was their ruler but it was difficult for them to follow a leader they could not see. They wanted a king like other nations who would help them in their battles. In telling the story emphasise that Saul was chosen by God and the anointing by Samuel was a sign of Saul being set apart by God to do a special job. This job has specific responsibilities.

A sovereign game

Ask the children to sit in a ring. Explain that the game is like pass the parcel. Play the regal music. While the music is playing the children must pass the crown around. When the music stops the child holding the crown is the king or queen. That child wears the crown and then stands up in the centre of the ring. The two children on either side of the new sovereign then present a bowl full of pieces of paper with instructions for what a sovereign must do. The child chooses a piece of paper and carries out the instructions. If possible let every child have a turn as sovereign.

After the game ask the children whether they expected the sovereign to do ordinary jobs as well as the more exciting ones? How should a king or queen have responsibility for his or her people? What sort of person does God want a ruler to be?

Regulations for kingship

In this activity the children have to consider what skills a king needs. Just as Samuel wrote down the rights and duties of kingship (1 Samuel 10 v25) the children can make their own scrolls to write down these rights and duties.

Drama

- Before the session read the story of how Saul is made king and work out a way you could act out the part of Samuel and retell the story through his eyes.

- In the session act out the story and ask the children to be the people and shout 'We want a King!'

- Choose at the appropriate moment for one of the children to be Saul. Tell Saul what to do as you tell the story. Emphasise Samuel's reliance on God and his acceptance that there must be a king even though he is not happy with it. Remind the group why Samuel was a good leader and explain why it was important that the new king Saul would need to know his subjects well.

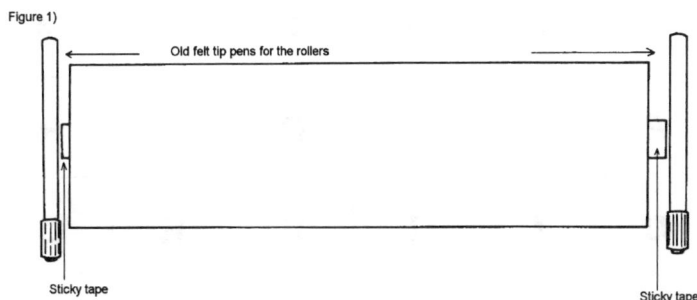

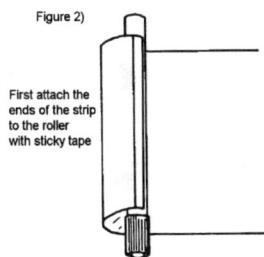

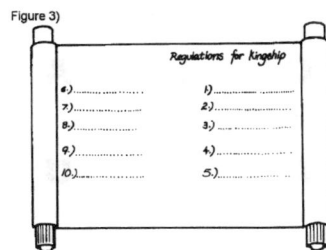

Figure 1)
Old felt tip pens for the rollers
Sticky tape
Sticky tape

Figure 2)
First attach the ends of the strip to the roller with sticky tape

Figure 3)
Regulations for Kingship
6).............. 1)..............
7).............. 2)..............
8).............. 3)..............
9).............. 4)..............
10).............. 5)..............

Figure 4)
Roll the scroll up and tie with the ribbon to hold together

A kingship scroll

You will need for each child
2 old felt tip pens
a piece of A4 paper folded in half lengthwise
    and cut in half
sticky tape
a length of narrow ribbon
drawing materials

Discuss with the group what Samuel might have written in the book which described the rights and duties of kingship (1 Samuel 10 v25). Write these down for use on an overhead projector or on a large sheet of paper or blackboard. They might include:

* someone who is just and fair

* someone who listens to his people

* someone who follows God's ways

* someone who cares for the people he leads

* someone who will treat people with respect and expect respect from his people

* someone who will allow God to help them do their work

The group can then write these rights and duties down on a scroll. Explain that a scroll was a long strip of parchment on which the writing was laid out in columns. The words written in Hebrew were read from right to left.

Each end of the parchment was fixed to a roller so that the text could be rolled up as it was read.

To make a simple model of a scroll

* Lay the paper strip flat on the table and attach each end to the felt-tip pen with sticky tape.

* Ask the children to write their regulations for kingship inside the roll.

* Finally roll the scroll up and tie up the scroll with the ribbon.

* The group can then take it in turns to read out the duties to their friends.

All age

A wordsearch
This wordsearch reminds the group when people were anointed in the Bible and when they are anointed today.

Preparation
Make enough copies of the wordsearch for each child to have a copy.

Ask a member of your church who uses oil for anointing to come along and explain what it is and how they use it.

Discussion
Samuel anointed Saul with oil to show that God had chosen him to be king. He poured the oil on

C	H	R	I	S	M	P	O	U	C
P	M	Y	R	R	H	R	N	N	I
O	L	I	V	E	O	I	L	C	N
W	A	S	A	M	U	E	L	T	N
C	C	A	N	E	Q	S	S	I	A
A	V	U	R	N	U	T	Z	O	M
S	O	L	O	M	O	N	S	N	O
S	E	B	A	P	T	I	S	M	N
I	R	S	X	E	L	I	S	H	A
A	M	T	M	E	S	S	I	A	H

Saul's head. Objects in the temple were also anointed to show that they were to serve God in a special way.

Using the themes section describe how holy oil is used in anointing today. Ask a priest or member of your church to explain to the group how they use oil in their ministry today. The children will want to see the oil and find out how it is administered. Perhaps someone who has been anointed could explain what happened and what it felt like.

The children can then look up the following Biblical references and work out these clues on anointing. Mark the answers in the wordsearch. Here are the solutions:

C	H	R	I	S	M	P	O	U	C
P	M	Y	R	R	H	R	N	N	I
O	L	I	V	E	O	I	L	C	N
W	A	S	A	M	U	E	L	T	N
C	C	A	N	E	Q	S	S	I	A
A	V	U	R	N	U	T	Z	O	M
S	O	L	O	M	O	N	S	N	O
S	E	B	A	P	T	I	S	M	N
I	R	S	X	E	L	I	S	H	A
A	M	T	M	E	S	S	I	A	H

1 What was Aaron to be anointed as in Exodus 28 v41?

2 What are the five ingredients of the holy oil listed in Exodus 30 v23-24 (RSV)?

3 Who was anointed in 1 Samuel 10 v1?

4 Who anointed King David in 1 Samuel 16 v13?

5 The king who was wise in 1 Kings 1 v39.

6 Who was Elijah to anoint as a prophet in 1 Kings 19 v16?

7 Jesus was the Anointed One, the Christos in Greek. What is the Hebrew name for the Anointed One?

8 At what sacrament do people receive holy oil and are welcomed into the Christian family?

9 What is another name for holy oil?

10 What is another name for anointing sick people, or those who are approaching death, with holy oil?

WORSHIP
Theme: Asking for God's guidance for our leaders

A prayer for our leaders
Ask the children to help you write a list of people who are leaders in their local community, in Britain and in the world. Then ask them what they think would be right to pray for them, e.g. that they will be fair and just; that they will listen to others, etc. They can then compose a prayer for the leaders they have chosen.

A state prayer
Almighty God, the fountain of all goodness, bless our Sovereign Lady, Queen Elizabeth, and all who are in authority under her; that they may order all things in wisdom and equity, righteousness and peace, to the honour of your name, and the good of your Church and people; through Jesus Christ our Lord. Amen.
ASB p103

Song suggestions
King of kings and Lord of lords (JP148)
The king of love my shepherd is (AMNS126, EH490, JP241)
Christ is the king! O friends rejoice (AMNS345)
King of glory, king of peace (AMNS194, EH424)
Hail to the Lord's anointed (AMNS142, EH45)

David and Goliath
1 Samuel 17

Themes
David's zeal and trust
David rose to Goliath's challenge because he was fighting for the reputation of Israel's God. This zeal is accompanied by an unfailing trust that God would make his people victorious. 'The Lord who delivered me from the paw of the lion and from the paw of the bear, will deliver me from the hand of this Philistine.' (1 Samuel 17 v37, RSV).

Fearlessness
The Israelites are afraid of Goliath. They see his size and his superior strength and are frightened. But David believes that God is with him and his trust leads to a fearlessness in the face of danger.

God is powerful
David fights without armour. His youth and inexperience is contrasted with Goliath's huge frame and armour. The fight shows that the God of Israel is far from powerless against his enemies. Even a young man is able to overcome the most fearsome giant with God's help.

ASB links
Pentecost 9 Year Two

Did you know?
The Philistines were a great enemy of Israel. They too were settlers in the land of Canaan. It is believed the ancient Philistines were sea peoples, possibly from the islands in the Aegean sea who settled in the Canaanite coastal towns of Gaza, Ashkelon, Ashdod, Ekron and Gath. The Philistines knew how to make iron and so their weapons were stronger than those of their enemies.

Bible quotation
Then David said to the Philistine, 'You come to me with a sword and with a spear and with a javelin; but I come to you in the name of the Lord of hosts, the God of the armies of Israel, whom you have defied.'
Samuel 17 v45, RSV

David was a shepherd and the youngest son of Jesse. Three of David's brothers were fighting on the side of Israel against the Philistines. Fighting for the Philistines was Goliath, a great giant who challenged the Israelites to find a man to fight him and kill him. When David visited his brothers to take them food, he heard of Goliath's challenge. His brothers and the rest of King Saul's men fled from Goliath but David rose to the challenge, 'For who is this uncircumcised Philistine, that he should defy the armies of the living God?' (1 Samuel 17 v26, RSV). David appeared before King Saul who doubted whether the young David was able to fight the giant. David told Saul about his conquests with lions and bears in protecting his sheep. Saul relented and gave David a coat of armour. But David was not used to armour and took it off. Instead he took only his staff and five smooth stones and a sling to fight Goliath. Goliath mocked his young challenger. But David told Goliath that God was on his side. With his sling and stones David struck Goliath on the forehead. The great giant fell and was killed. David then cut off Goliath's head. When the rest of the Philistine army saw that Goliath was dead they took flight and the Israelites were victorious.

ACTIVITIES

Younger children

Goliath skittles
As a shepherd boy David had learnt many skills including that of defending himself against lions and bears. When he fought animals he trusted that God would be with him. As he faced the giant Goliath he again put his trust in God and used the skills God had given him. Young children also have skills which after much practice can be used for good.

Story
Retell the story of David and Goliath and emphasise the skills David had learnt as a shepherd boy. In Old Testament times a shepherd would have carried oil to heal the sheep's wounds or scratches, a club to drive off wild animals that kill sheep, a staff to guide sheep and lift them out of dangerous places and a sling for hurling stones at wild animals. He must have spent many hours practising the use of his sling and hitting targets at a distance. He told Saul that he had killed bears and lions.

David also had a kinnor or harp which he learnt to play and made up songs while watching the sheep.

Discussion
Ask the children what skills they have learnt. Perhaps they can run fast, skip or ride a bike. Discuss with them the different stages of learning to ride a bike or learning to swim. Like David these skills can be used for good.

This skittle activity provides a safer alternative to using a sling and reminds the children how David knocked down Goliath.

To make a Goliath skittle you will need
plastic drink bottles
newspaper
sand
funnel
paste
wool
foil
paint
tennis balls

In the session the children can each make a skittle:

- Fill the plastic bottle a quarter full with sand, using the funnel. The sand will help the bottle stand upright.
- Make Goliath's head by crumpling up a sheet of newspaper into a head shape with a piece for the neck.
- Push the neck piece into the top of the bottle.
- Paste newspaper strips all over the bottle and the head to cover the whole shape. Allow to dry.
- Paint the face and use the wool to make hair.
- Paint the body brown to represent a tunic.
- Make a helmet and breastplate out of foil and attach it to the Goliath model.

Once the skittles are completed all the children play the game.

A drama of David and Goliath

Older children

David was fearless and put his trust in God. Through acting out this role play the children can experience something of David's courage.

You will need
props or materials to make them
card
pencils

Discussion
Retell the story and encourage the children to imagine what each of the characters felt like. Then ask them all to walk round the room and be a worried and frightened King Saul, a fearless and confident David, a tall, brutal Goliath, and a frightened group of soldiers. Then find out who would like to be each of the main characters in the story.

Drama
You will need props which make it obvious who the children are. The children can make the props: a **crown** for King Saul, **swords** for the soldiers, a **sling and newspaper balls** for David and a child standing behind a **large cardboard cut-out Goliath**. Encourage the group to act out the story without a script. Then ask them to write out the key phrases of the story on cards. The group can now act out the story again using the phrase cards. If the group goes on to do a public performance of the drama these cards may provide the outline of the script.

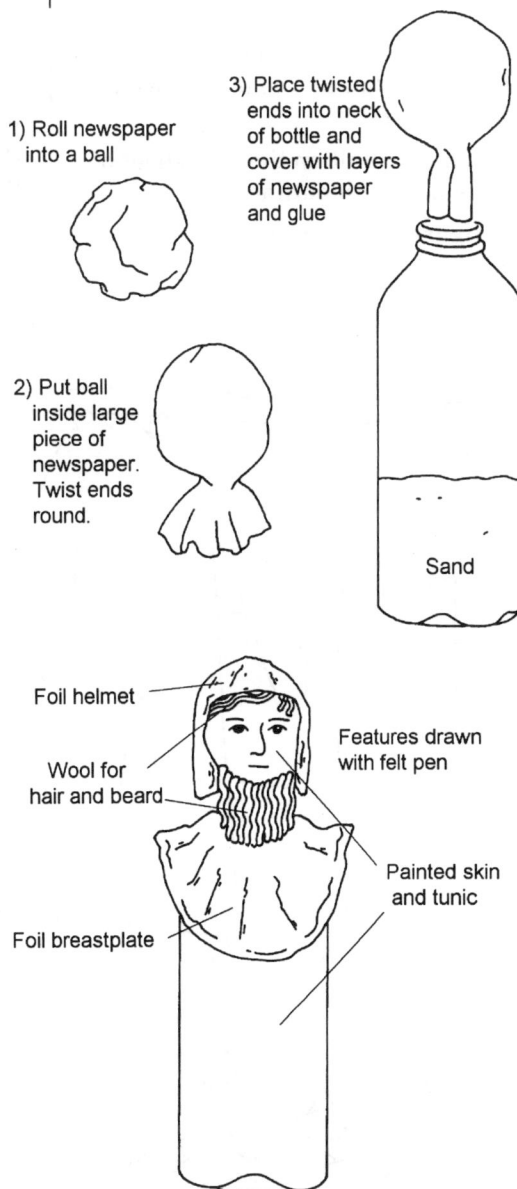

1) Roll newspaper into a ball

2) Put ball inside large piece of newspaper. Twist ends round.

3) Place twisted ends into neck of bottle and cover with layers of newspaper and glue

Sand

Foil helmet

Features drawn with felt pen

Wool for hair and beard

Painted skin and tunic

Foil breastplate

59

A tower of fears

All age

The David and Goliath story shows that God is not powerless against fearful enemies. It is normal for children to have fears and worries. The leader can explain how faith and trust in God can sometimes help people overcome fear. If possible they can give some practical examples.

You will need
large cardboard boxes which can be stacked
felt-tip pens
a large sheet of paper the size of a tall adult
sticky address labels
scissors
glue
soft balls

Retell the story and then discuss with the group what they find frightening. It could be darkness, fear of being run over, fear of drowning, fear of family break up, fear of a bully, fear of war or famine, fire or hardship. Ask the children to

- Write down each fear on the back of a cardboard box.
- Stack all the boxes into a tower as tall as an adult, making sure that all the fears are on one face of the tower.
- Draw around a tall adult on the long sheet of paper to make a Goliath outline.
- Cut out the figure and glue on the reverse.

- Carefully stick this figure onto the opposite side of the 'tower of fears'.
- On the soft balls stick a sticky label with the words 'God is powerful'.

The children can now throw balls at Goliath until he falls down. Show how the children's fears which are written on the other side of the boxes have also fallen down.

WORSHIP
Prayer
Blow up a balloon and write on it with a permanent felt tip pen the fears the children have. Then say this prayer with them:

Father God, help us all not to be overwhelmed by fear. Protect us from those things which we find frightening so, like David, we can trust that you will be with us always. Amen.

Then take a pin and burst the balloon to illustrate that God can get rid of all our fears.

Song suggestions
There he stood Goliath (JP475)
Stand up, stand up for Jesus (AMNS221, EH581, JP226)
When a knight won his spurs (CP50)
Be strong and courageous (SOF9)
Who would true valour see (AMNS212)
Only a boy called David (JP190)

David the music-maker

Themes

David had many gifts

David had been given many gifts by God. He was a skilful shepherd and an accomplished musician. His gift of music made him a popular figure in King Saul's court. He played the lyre and sang songs.

Music to praise God

The stories of David in the books of Samuel and 1 Chronicles show how music was used to sing praise to God. Many of the Psalms attributed to David are hymns of praise to God.

Music and dancing

Singing and dancing feature in many of the David stories. When David returned home victorious after fighting the Philistines the people sang and danced.

In 2 Samuel 6 when the people brought the ark to Jerusalem David and all the Israelites made merry before the Lord and David danced before the Lord with all his might.

King David was a great king, soldier, poet and musician. In 1 Samuel he is described as 'A son of Jesse the Bethlehemite, who is skilful in playing, a man of valour, a man of war, prudent in speech, and a man of good presence; and the Lord is with him.' (1 Samuel 16 v18, RSV). He was an accomplished musician and played the lyre for King Saul when the King was tormented with an evil spirit.

David is often thought of as the Psalmist. The Psalms, a collection of 150 hymns, poems and prayers can be grouped in different ways and were written at different times in Israel's history. Seventy three of them are attributed to David.

The Psalms express every kind of human emotion before God who is involved in all aspects of life. Today the Psalms play an important part in both Jewish and Christian worship.

ACTIVITIES

Younger children

Psalm 23

Psalm 23 is one of the most popular psalms. David uses the image of God as a shepherd. Jesus also uses this image of a good shepherd of himself (John 10 v11). The theme of a caring shepherd can be explored with children by creating a musical setting of Psalm 23.

Before the session

Find a children's adaptation of Psalm 23 (these story books are helpful: *The Lord is my Shepherd* by Kersten Hamilton (Chariot Books), *Sometimes I get scared – Psalm 23 for children* by Elspeth Campbell (Pickering and Inglis). Find a song or hymn version of Psalm 23.

Collect dressing up clothes and props for a shepherd including a walking stick, a rod, a container with oil, a bag with food in (cheese, dates, figs, grapes and pitta bread, a flask of water).

For the activity provide a variety of children's musical instruments: shakers, drums, triangles, kazoos, bells, cymbals etc.

In the session

The leader should dress up in the shepherd's costume. As Psalm 23 is read or sung point out to the children what it tells us about the work of a shepherd. A shepherd takes his sheep from place to place in search of fresh pasture and fresh water. He leads the sheep onto

61

the right paths by calling them. The sheep know his voice. He has a staff or crook to control the sheep. His rod or club is used to fight wild animals off. He carries oil attached to his belt to heal wounded sheep.

Making music
Show the children the different musical instruments and ask them what kind of music they can make with each one. Can they make quiet, soft sounds or noisy, joyful ones? Can the instrument be played quickly or slowly? Does it make high sounds or low sounds? What do the different sounds make them feel like?

Read the Psalm through again but this time stop and ask them to suggest ways of providing music for the different passages.

- v1-3 Quiet lullaby music for 'lie down in green pastures', and 'still waters'.
- v4 Fearful music for 'the valley of the shadow of death', bold strong music for 'I fear no evil'.
- v5 Happy joyful music for 'Thou preparest a table before me'.
- v6 Calm happy music for 'Surely goodness and mercy shall follow me all the days of my life'. (RSV)

If there is time try putting it all together for the worship time.

An acrostic psalm

Older children

Psalm 34 is an acrostic psalm. In the Hebrew each line begins with the consecutive letter of the Hebrew alphabet beginning with the first letter. Psalm 34 has 22 lines because there are 22 letters in the Hebrew alphabet. This great hymn of praise is attributed to David.

T
H
A
N
K

Discuss with the group times when they have been thankful – for a new brother or sister, for Christmas, for friends, for winning at football, for receiving a present etc. Ask the children to write their own hymn of praise to express their gratefulness to God. They can make an acrostic psalm by using the letters in THANK YOU.

Y
O
U

All age

Singing and dancing

The people of Israel sang and danced when the Ark of the Covenant was brought into Jerusalem. The singing and dancing was to honour God. Jubilate Deo means 'praise God'.

Psalm 100 is a hymn of praise to God. Although it is not attributed to David it is a psalm that has a number of modern musical adaptations. This activity encourages children to use singing and dancing to praise God.

Before the session
Find a musical version of Psalm 100. As well as the traditional chant used at Morning Prayer there are two Taizé versions and a song, *Jubilate, Everybody* (JP145).

In the session
Explain that King David and the Israelites sang and danced to honour God.

- Teach the group Psalm 100 to the setting you have chosen. You can try singing the psalm antiphonally, i.e. with one of two groups singing alternate verses.

- Ask the children to work out suitable actions and steps to the music and words.

WORSHIP
Theme: Celebrating and giving thanks to God for his love

Include in the worship the activity work done by the group.

Prayer
Lord God, we come singing, dancing and making music, to thank you for your great love and care. Like David, who danced and leapt for joy, so we sing your praises and worship you. Amen.

Song suggestions
Come let us sing for joy (Ps95) (JP324)
Come let us sing for joy (Ps95) (SOF16)
Sing a new song to the Lord (Ps98) (JP454)
We'll praise him on the trumpet (JP486)
Praise the Lord in everything! (CP33)
O praise ye the Lord (Ps150) (AMNS203, CP37)

On Psalm 23
Surely Goodness and mercy (JP223)
The Lord's my shepherd (JP243, CP56, AMNS426)
The king of love (AMNS126, CP54, EH490, JP241)
The Lord is my shepherd (JP244)
The God of love my shepherd is (AMNS110, EH93)
The Lord my pasture shall prepare (AMNS111, EH491)

On Psalm 100
Before Jehovah's awful throne (AMNS197)
All people that on earth do dwell (AMNS100, EH365, JP4)

Solomon's Temple
1 Kings 5-6

Themes

Offering the best to God
Nothing but the best wood, stones and decoration would do for the Temple which Solomon built to worship God.

Holy place
The Ark of the Covenant which contained the tablets of stone of the ten commandments, was a special holy object to the people of Israel. When the Temple was built the Ark was housed in the inner sanctuary, the Holy of holies. Throughout history people have set aside special places to worship God.

Temples of God
Solomon recognised that God could not be contained in a temple, however great. In his first letter to the Corinthians St Paul says that people are God's temple because God dwells in them. (1 Corinthians 3 v16)

ASB links
Epiphany 4 Year One

Bible quotation
Then in the presence of the people Solomon went and stood in front of the altar, where he raised his arms and prayed, 'Lord God of Israel, there is no god like you in heaven above or on earth below! You keep your covenant with your people and show them your love when they live in whole-hearted obedience to you.'
1 Kings 8 v22-23, GNB

During the reign of Solomon Israel was a rich and stable nation at peace with its neighbours. King Solomon carried out his father, King David's plans to build a temple for the worship of God. Solomon asked Hiram, King of Tyre, to provide cedars of Lebanon and cypress timber for the building. Thousands of men were conscripted into forced labour to chop the trees and to quarry stone for the foundation of the new Temple. 1 Kings 5-6 gives details of the building: it was made from stone and inside the walls were lined with wood carved into the shapes of flowers, palm-trees and cherubim overlaid with gold. An inner sanctuary was built to house the Ark of the Covenant.

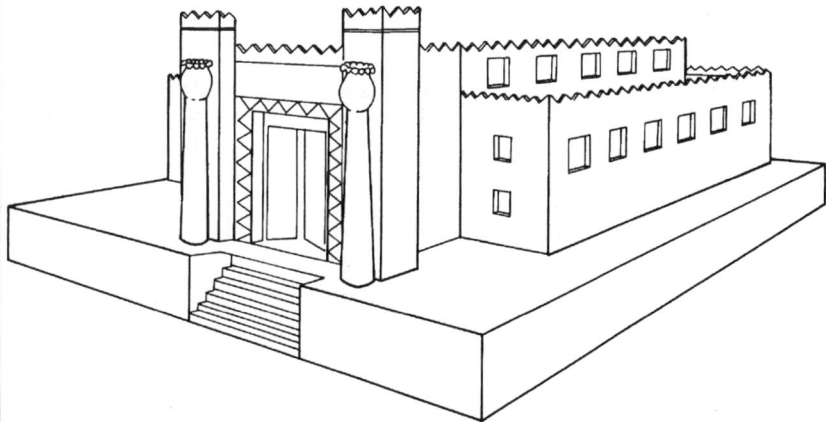

The Temple took seven years to build. When it was completed King Solomon, accompanied by the priests and leaders of Israel, brought the Ark of the Covenant into the inner sanctuary. The Temple was filled with a cloud and God's presence filled the building: 'You, Lord, have placed the sun in the sky, yet you have chosen to live in clouds and darkness. Now I have built a majestic temple for you, a place for you to live in for ever.' (1 Kings 8 v12-13, GNB).

The Temple became the centre of worship for the people of Israel until it was destroyed by King Nebuchadnezzar of Babylon in 587 BC.

ACTIVITIES
Telling the story
Tell the children that King Solomon wanted to build a wonderful temple where people could go and worship God. He recruited people with special skills and used the best materials possible to create a magnificent place of worship. Encourage the children to help you tell the story.

- King Solomon sent men to collect cedars and cypresses (pine trees) from Lebanon. King Hiram of Tyre was asked by Solomon to provide his people to help the Israelites cut the trees down. The children can mime felling trees and at a given sign shout 'TIMBER!' (1 Kings 5 v6-8).

- King Hiram's men took the logs down to the sea and tied them into rafts to float down the coast. The children can mime sitting on the rafts with a paddle saying 'Dip, dip and swing', as they move their paddles from side to side in unison (1 Kings 5 v9).

- Men worked in the hill country quarrying stone and then the stones were dressed at the quarry so that there was no noise made by tools at the Temple. The children can pretend to hold a hammer and a chisel and say 'Hammer, hammer, chip, hammer, hammer, chip.' (1 Kings 5 v15-18, 6 v7).

- The inside of the Temple was covered in gold. It was decorated with carved figures of winged creatures, palm trees and flowers all covered in gold. The children can become winged creatures, palm trees and flowers and when the leader hits a triangle they can become a still golden statue (1 Kings 6).

- A master craftsman cast two bronze columns eight metres tall to stand at the entrance of the Temple. He also made many objects for use in the Temple. They were made of polished bronze. The children can mime rubbing and polishing (1 Kings 7 v15).

- When the Temple was finished there was a great ceremony and King Solomon stood in front of the altar and stretching his hands to heaven he said, 'O Lord, God of Israel, etc.' (see Bible quotation). Ask the children to raise their hands above their heads and repeat Solomon's words after you.

Painting an altar cloth

Younger children

Solomon employed all the best craftsmen to build and decorate the Temple where his people could worship God. The children can offer their best to God by using their creative skills in designing and painting an altar cloth.

You will need
an old bed sheet large enough to cover the table used during worship
ready-mixed paint
paint brushes
soft (B) pencils
rubbers
plastic sheeting to protect the floor
children's aprons

After telling the story ask the children what they like to do to say thank you to someone they love. Would they give a present; share some sweets or special toy; write a thank you letter; give a kiss and a cuddle or provide a special treat? Solomon loved God so much that he wanted to build a Temple where God could be worshipped. Tell the children that they are going to make something to say thank you to

God. What they make will be beautiful like Solomon's Temple and will help people worship God.

Activity
Explain to the children that they are going to make an altar cloth. On the cloth they will paint pictures which express their thanks to God. Can they think of things which they can say thank you to God for? Perhaps friends, pets, flowers, family, sunshine and rain?

- Help each child to choose something they can draw and paint on the cloth.

- Sketch the drawing on the cloth with a pencil and when the children are happy with the pencil outline they can paint the cloth.

Holy places

Older children

The Temple was a holy place where God could be worshipped. Within the Temple there was an inner sanctuary, the Holy of holies where the Ark of the Covenant was kept (1 Kings 6 v15ff). These activities explore the theme of holy places.

Making a model of the Temple
This is a peep-through box so that children can look into a model Temple. The group make a very detailed model of the Temple by adding details to this simple plan.

You will need
a shoe box
gold paper or card
greaseproof paper
birthday candle holders
modelling material
paper
glue
spreaders
a matchbox
cocktail sticks
scissors
glue

1 Line the inside of the shoe box with gold paper.

2 Cut out the front door of the Temple.

3 At the opposite end to the door make a gold screen the width of the box. Cut out a central door in the screen as shown.

4 Attach the screen to make a 'Holy of holies'.

5 Place two symmetrical rows of modelling material in the main Temple as shown.

6 Press the ten candle holders through these to create the ten lampstands.

7 Make a simple gold altar and a gold table for the bread of Presence. The bread can be made from small pieces of white paper.

Cherubim

cocktail sticks

matchbox

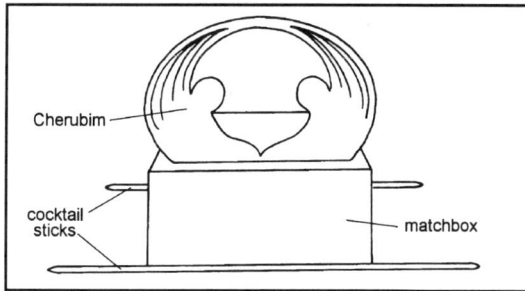

8 To make the Ark of the Covenant, cover a matchbox with gold paper, cut out the cherubim shape as shown and attach to the top of the box. Stick cocktail sticks along the bottom edges of the box as shown to make the carrying poles.

9 Stick the 'Ark' in the 'Holy of holies'.

10 Make the two large cherubim from pieces of gold card and attach to the floor of the 'Holy of holies'.

11 Cover the top of the box with greasproof paper.

screen

candle holder

tables

Front door cut out

greaseproof paper lid

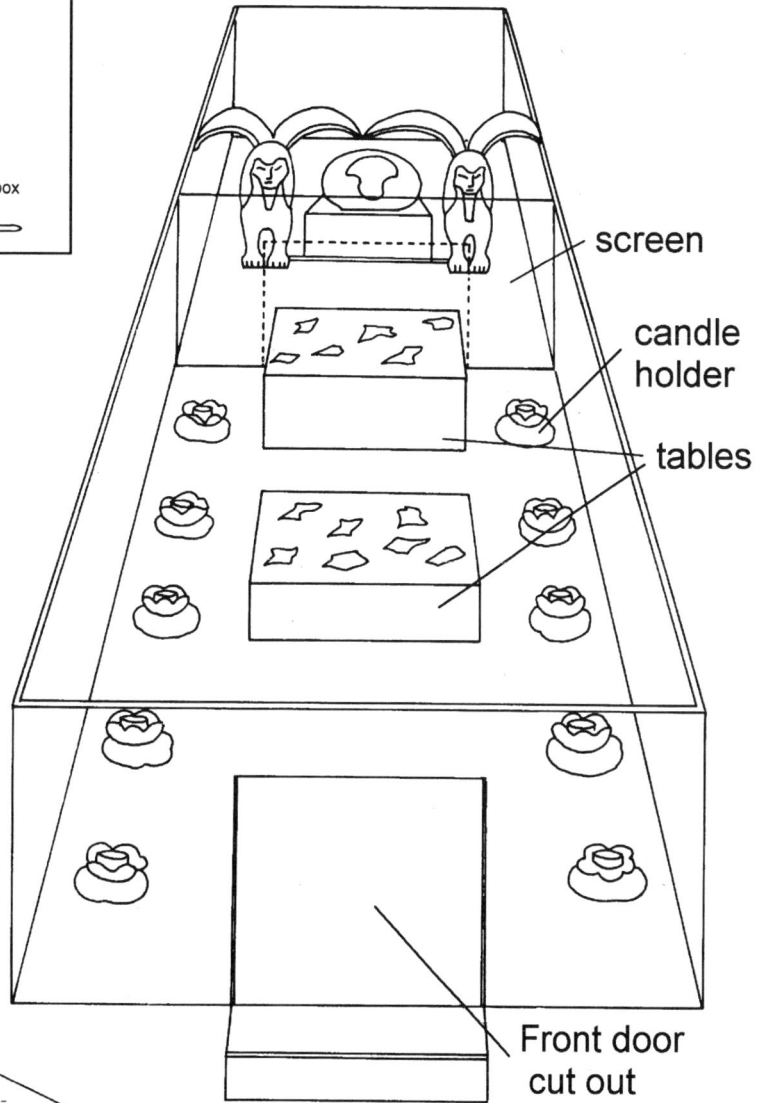

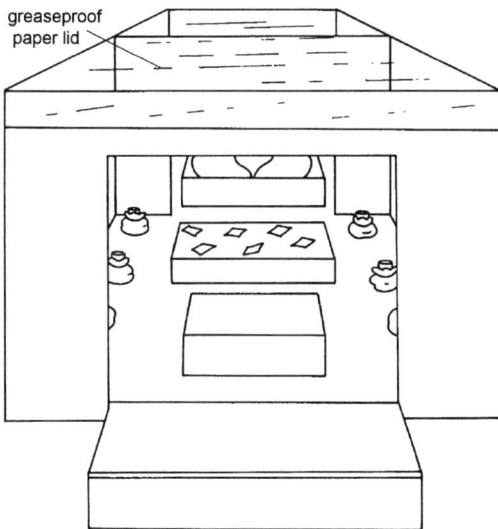

What makes a place holy?

All age

Collect materials to make one or several of these craft activities.

To make small flower arrangements you will need
foil dishes
oasis cut to fit and soaked in water
flowers
scissors
newspaper to cover the table

To decorate candles you will need
baptism candles
non-inflammable materials such as sequins and foil pieces
PVA glue

To decorate a verse from the Bible you will need
one copy of Solomon's prayer (1 Kings 6 v23) copied onto paper for each child
pencil crayons or felt-tip pens to decorate

To make a small cross you will need
straight sticks (two for each cross)
string to bind them together

To make an icon you will need
a selection of Christmas cards or postcards of religious subjects
card to stick pictures onto
scissors
glue

• After telling the story of the building of Solomon's Temple discuss with the children where they worship God; in church, at school, at home and sometimes even outside.

- What helps to make it a 'holy' place where the presence of God is encountered? It could be the building, the silence, music and singing, candles, a cross, stained glass windows, dimness, incense, an altar or communion table, an icon, a verse from the Bible, or some event which led to an understanding of God.

- Tell the children about the different things they can make which may help them worship God. Help each child to decide what they will make from the list given.

- Use the objects the children have created in the worship and then encourage them to take them back home to make a place for prayer at home.

WORSHIP
Theme: Thanking God for his presence in our worship

Preparation
Make a table the focal point for worship and place on it the altar cloth (if dry enough), the flower arrangements, a tin full of sand to place the candles in and the crosses stuck into a plasticine base. Behind the table use Blu-Tack to put up the 'icons' and Bible verses.

Prayer
Ask the children to place the candles in the sand so that the leader can light them.

Lord God, Father of us all, we thank you and give you praise for the creative gifts we have used to make these things today. Help us to know your presence with us now and always. Amen.

Song suggestions
The building song (CP61)
We love the place, O God (AMNS160, EH508)
Christ is our corner-stone (AMNS161)
God is love (CP36)
Thank you, Lord (CP32)
All over the world (JP5)
For I'm building a people of power (JP47)
Lord, the light of your love (SOF127)
Give me oil in my lamp (JP50, SOF39)
Standing in your presence Lord (JP466)

Elijah hears a still small voice

1 Kings 19

Themes

God meets people's needs

The story of Elijah shows how God cares for his people and the special prophets he chooses. God anticipates Elijah's needs and shows his power through him.

God speaks through prophets

God chooses many different sorts of people to be his messengers. Prophets like Elijah 'speak out' on God's behalf. Their message is often unpopular and they are often persecuted as Elijah was.

God as a still small voice

After showing his power through controlling the weather, sending a fire and providing food and drink for Elijah, God reveals himself in a still small voice.

ASB links

5 before Christmas Year One

Bible quotation

And behold, the Lord passed by, and a great and strong wind rent the mountains, and broke in pieces the rocks before the Lord, but the Lord was not in the wind; and after the wind an earthquake, but the Lord was not in the earthquake; and after the earthquake a fire, but the Lord was not in the fire; and after the fire a still small voice.
1 Kings 19 v11-12, RSV

Elijah was a prophet chosen by God. Elijah lived during the reign of Ahab (c.869-850 BC). At this time the people of Israel had split into two kingdoms, Israel in the North and Judah in the South. King Ahab's wife, Jezebel was the daughter of a Tyrian king who was also a priest of Baal. Ahab had built a temple to Baal and many in his kingdom followed this god and turned away from God.

Elijah (his name means Yahweh is God) was a man of God who prophesied to his people. God provided for Elijah and showed his power through the acts that Elijah performed. On one occasion Elijah called King Ahab and all the prophets of Baal and the people of Israel to Mount Carmel to a trial of power to see whether Baal or Yahweh would respond to his followers to send down fire to consume a sacrifice. The people did as Elijah had asked but no fire appeared on the sacrifice to Baal. Then Elijah set up an altar and soaked it in water. He called on God to show himself to his people. The fire fell and the people believed. Elijah then killed the prophets of Baal. When Jezebel heard of this she threatened to kill Elijah. Elijah escaped to the wilderness and prayed to God that he might die. An angel touched him and told him to eat a cake and drink that was provided. Elijah ate and drank and lay down again. Again an angel touched him and told him to eat as the journey would be too great for him. He arose and ate and then spent 40 days on Mount Horeb.

On Horeb he lived in a cave and the word of God came to him. There, after experiencing a great wind, an earthquake, and a fire he heard God's message to him in a still small voice. God told him to anoint Hazael to be king over Syria and Jehu to be king of Israel and to anoint Elisha to be prophet in his place.

ACTIVITIES

Younger children

God does not fail his people

Through this story children can learn that God knew when Elijah was sad, lonely and depressed and God met his needs. The children need not always say happy things to God but share their sadness too. God can turn sadness to joy.

You will need

partly cooked potatoes for heads (soft enough to put cocktail sticks in easily)
strips of red and yellow pepper to make happy and sad mouth shapes
sliced carrot for ears
sultanas for eyes
glace cherries or small soft sweets for noses
parsley, lettuce, cress or fennel leaf for hair
cocktail sticks cut in half

Tell the story of Elijah (1 Kings 19). Ask the children to make the appropriate facial gesture at each point in the story.

- When he ran away from Queen Jezebel (v3). Ask the children to look afraid.

- When he rested under the broom tree and asked God to let him die (v4). Ask the children to look hungry and then go to sleep.

- When the angel provided food (v5-8). Ask the children to show surprise.

- When Elijah talks to God (v10 and 14). Ask the children to show anger and sadness.

- When Elijah waits for God to come during the wind, earthquake, and fire (v11,12). Ask the children to show that they are listening and waiting.

- When Elijah goes out to God (v13). Ask the children to cover their faces.

- When God tells Elijah what to do (v15-18). Ask the children to show relief and happiness.

Elijah felt many emotions during the time when he had to run for his life. He must have wondered what God was doing. Even when Elijah felt despair, God met his needs and empowered him to act.

Make a potato face Elijah
Hand out one potato for each child and ask them to make a happy face on one side and a sad face on the other using the fruit, sweets and vegetables. Help the children to secure the different foods with half a cocktail stick, pressing the sharp end into the potato.

Standing up for what you believe in
Older children

The story of Elijah and the prophets of Baal shows Elijah standing up for what he believes in despite of the consequences. Elijah trusted that God would not fail him even though his prophetic message was unpopular. The children may well feel strongly about some issues and this might be an opportunity for them to speak about them to the group.

Preparation
You will need to know what children in your group are concerned about before the session. Issues may include local environmental matters, animal abuse, bullying at school, street children, unfairness of referees at school matches or a pop group issue. Ask children to bring along to the session articles or handouts about issues they are interested in.

You will need
cut-out letters to the editor or articles from children's magazines
school newsletters
national newspapers and magazines
letter handouts from the template below
drawing materials

Tell the story of Elijah and the prophets of Baal (1 Kings 18 v20-46) and show how Elijah was not afraid to stand up for what he believed. Ask the children to share with each other the concerns some of them have. In twos and threes read some of the articles and letters. Do they agree or disagree with them? Why do people feel like this? Would it be something God would care about?

A letter of concern
Encourage each child or groups of two children to write a letter for the church magazine or to someone in the community. Give each group a letter to fill in and ask if they mind if it goes in the newsletter. Read the letters to each other afterwards.

St. .... Sunday School

Dear ....

We are writing this letter because we are concerned about...
....

We feel that you should be aware of ......
.....

We feel that the situation could be improved if .....
......

yours sincerely....
......

A powerful God

All age

Children are surrounded by powerful things: cars, computers, television, pop music, famous people etc. Remind the group that none of these is as powerful as God and none can love them as God does. God's power is not necessarily shown in the things people find powerful but is sometimes shown in a 'still small voice'.

You will need
a large sheet of paper
catalogues
magazines
scissors
a marker pen
glue
spreaders

Tell the story of Elijah from 1 Kings 19 v3-18. Before telling the story divide the children into five groups and give one group a picture of flames and another a picture of food. Ask the other groups to practise sound effects for rain and wind and actions for the earthquake. In telling the story emphasise God's power in sending fire, rain, in providing food and in sending the wind, earthquake and fire. Ask the children to show their pictures and do the sound effects and actions at the appropriate times.

God the creator who made us and the world we live in is all powerful. However Elijah found that it was in the still and quiet that God provided his needs. In the waiting before Christmas we remember God's love for us in sending his son Jesus to live on earth. Christians often experience God's love when they are still, quiet and at peace with themselves and not in the turmoil and business of the day.

A collage of power
Ask the children to cut out from the catalogues and magazines powerful things such as cars, hi-fi equipment, lamps, food mixers, rockets, televisions, volcanoes, hurricanes and fires. Stick them on to a large sheet of paper and over the top write 'God is in the still small voice'.

WORSHIP
Theme: God can turn our sorrow into action

Prayer
Almighty God, the all powerful creator of the earth, you chose not to speak to Elijah in the wind, earthquake or fire but in a still small voice. As you changed Elijah's sorrow and anger into action to work for you, so heal our sorrows that we might joyfully live and work to your praise and glory. Amen.

Song suggestions
The prophets spoke in days of old (AMNS513)
O worship the Lord in the beauty of holiness (AMNS49, EH42)
Be still and know that I am God (JP22)
Fill your hearts with joy (CP9)
Great is your faithfulness (JP64)
Dear Lord and father of mankind (AMNS115, EH383)

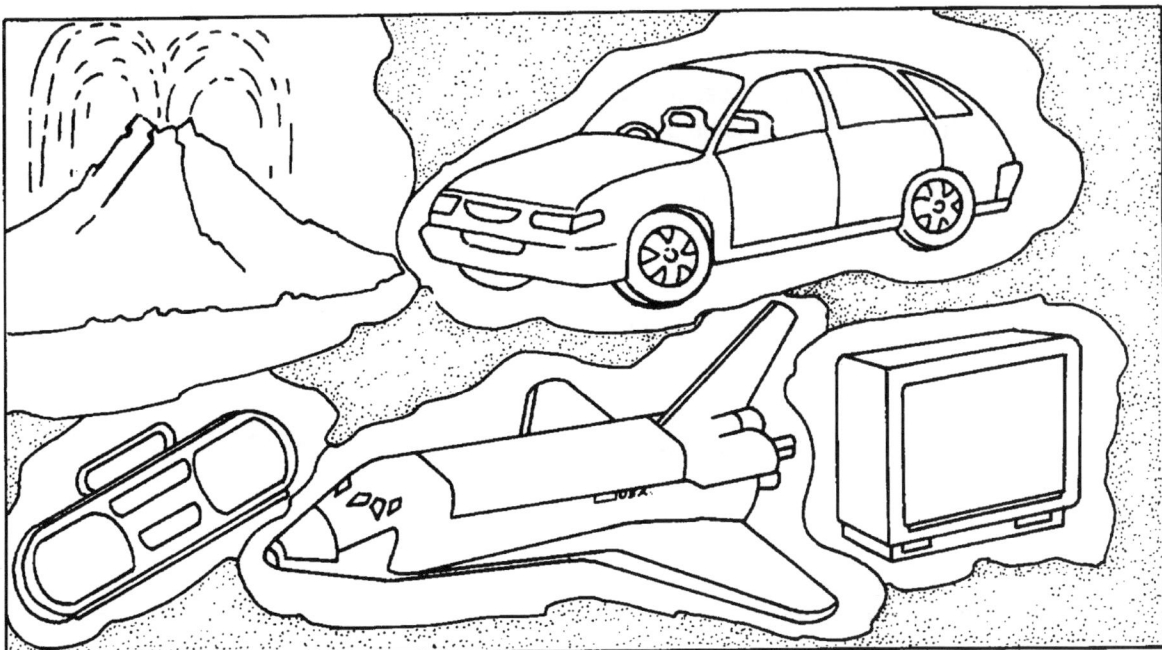

Naaman is cured
2 Kings 5 v1-14

Themes

God's ways are often unexpected

Naaman expected God to work like other gods: to use his special prophets to wave a magic wand and miraculously cure him. God's ways are often unexpected. They may seem incredible.

Leprosy

Leprosy sufferers throughout the ages have suffered discrimination. Today leprosy is curable but people still treat certain categories of people as 'lepers' in the same way, e.g. AIDS sufferers etc.

Healing

When God heals he may use many other people and events to help cure people. The prophets foretold a time when God's healing love would renew and restore. In his healing acts Jesus brings new life and restores people to wholeness. Healing need not just be physical healing but rather making a person whole. Naaman's disease is taken away from him by God working through Elisha. Naaman is also made whole because he recognises God for the first time.

ASB links

8 before Easter Year Two

Bible quotation

Behold, I thought that he would surely come out to me, and stand, and call on the name of the Lord his God, and wave his hand over the place, and cure the leper. Are not Abana and Pharpar, the rivers of Damascus, better than all the waters of Israel? Could I not wash in them and be clean?
2 Kings 5 v11-12, RSV

Point of information

Instead of using the word 'leper' which is often linked with uncleanliness and defilement it is better to describe Naaman as a 'leprosy sufferer' or 'leprosy victim'. The Leprosy Mission, Goldhay Way, Orton Goldhay, Peterborough, PE2 5GZ (Tel. 01733 370505) has information and resource material relevant to children which could provide a useful resource for these activities.

The books of 1 and 2 Kings are a record of the history of Israel from the close of David's reign to the fall of Jerusalem in 587 BC. The story of Naaman and Elisha is set at a time when there was peace between Israel and Syria.

Naaman was the commander of the King of Syria's army. Although he was a popular and successful man, he suffered from leprosy. On one of their raids the Syrians had captured an Israelite maid who served Naaman's wife. The maid said to her mistress that she wished that Naaman would see a prophet in Samaria who would cure him of his leprosy. The King of Syria gave Naaman permission to go to Israel and sent him with a letter for the King of Israel. When the King of Israel read the letter asking that Naaman be cured, he tore his clothes in anger because he thought the King of Syria was picking a quarrel with him.

When the prophet Elisha heard what had happened, he sent a messenger to Naaman and told him to go and wash in the Jordan seven times and he would be cured. Naaman received the message with anger because Elisha did not come in person to meet him, call upon God and wave his hand over him. He asked whether the Jordan was better than his own rivers to wash in. Naaman went away in a rage but his servants begged him to return. Naaman went and washed himself in the Jordan and his flesh was restored. Naaman went to Elisha and said 'Behold, I know that there is no God in all the earth but in Israel; so accept now a present from your servant.' (2 Kings 5 v15, RSV). Elisha would not accept the present.

ACTIVITIES
Healing links

The story of Naaman shows how God sometimes uses many people to help make people well. This drama helps illustrate the number of people who can help heal someone. As with leprosy sufferers, there is a physical illness as well as emotional and spiritual needs which have to be met to help make a person whole.

You will need
8 strips of paper, glue and drawing materials

Before the session
Write on the eight strips the names of the people who brought about Naaman's cure (Naaman, Naaman's maid, Naaman's wife, the King of Syria, the King of Israel, Elisha, Elisha's messenger and Naaman's servants).

In the session
- Tell the story of Naaman.

- While telling the story ask a different child to stand at the front and hold the strip of paper with the name of the character they are representing.

- As each subsequent name is mentioned ask different children to hold the strip with the name on of the person they are representing.

- Ask the children to link their arms to form a chain.

- At the end of the story point out how each person in the chain helped Naaman to get better.

- Ask the first child representing Naaman to stick the ends of the strip together to form a loop and then ask the others to link their strips in to form a chain.

- Point out how each link in the chain is important for the strength of the chain in the same way as each person in the story was important for the healing of Naaman.

Group acting – a short drama
This drama makes a similar point in a modern day setting.

Before the session
Collect together the props for the story: a toy phone, a bell, a toy doctor's bag, a bag with pyjamas, sponge bag and a teddy.

Select a group of children to improvise a short drama from this story outline.

A girl is playing outside with her friends and cannot hear when her father calls her in. Her father rings the surgery to make an appointment to see the doctor. The doctor gives her a hearing test. She goes to the hospital to see the hearing specialist who tells her that she must have a grommet fitted in her ear. At church she tells her friends that she does not want to have an operation in hospital. Her friends reassure her that she will not be alone. They will pray to Jesus and ask that he will be with her and with those who are helping her. In hospital the surgeon operates on her ear and afterwards she tells everyone how she can now hear a lot better and how she liked being in hospital. She and her friends say 'thank you' to Jesus when they are in church next Sunday.

Just as a chain of different people helped Naaman be healed so people today depend on a number of people to help them get better. The children can improvise similar stories for themselves.

Leprosy today
Through these activities the children will understand more about what leprosy is, how it affects people today and how leprosy sufferers return to everyday life.

After telling the story of Naaman explain to the group that the first sign of leprosy is usually patches on the skin (light patches on dark skin and red on light skin). Any person of any age can contract it. Often an adult or child will hide the patches because they do not want to be separated from their families. People often reject and avoid leprosy sufferers so that they become outcasts. No wonder Naaman wanted to be healed. Today leprosy is found mainly in Africa, Asia and South America. Leprosy damages nerves especially in the hands, feet and face. Nowadays there is a cure for leprosy as long as the disease is diagnosed early. One tablet a day can kill most of the leprosy germs within six months. However there may be irreparable damage done to nerves in hands, feet and face which means that a person can lose their sense of feeling and so have to be trained to avoid hazards such as burns and cuts on the skin.

Tell the children that they are going to do some activities which will help them to understand what a child with leprosy in the feet is taught.

- Many people around the world do not wear shoes. Tell the children to take their shoes and socks off and walk round the room.

- Ask them what they can feel and give them some things to walk over which have different textures e.g. sandpaper, gravel, a sheep skin rug, cotton wool, baking trays, milk bottle tops, tea towels and paper.

- Explain that a child with leprosy in her feet has no feeling there. She can walk on something sharp and not know she has injured her foot for several days. The cut may become septic or an ulcer might form.

- Ask the children to sit down and look at their feet. Children with leprosy in their feet are taught to wash their feet each day in water and clean any cuts or bruises. After washing they rub the skin on their foot with ointment to keep it supple. If there is a cut they have to put a dressing on it and not walk on the foot until it is healed.

- Children with leprosy are encouraged to wear sandals to protect their feet. They are often made from old car tyres. They have to be made so that they do not have any harsh edges that rub against the feet.

- The children can then make their own card sandals.

To make card sandals you will need
cardboard
scissors
drawing materials
ribbons or tape

- Ask the children to draw around their own feet on a piece of card.

- Leave a 1cm border around the foot shape and cut out two soles.

- Make the holes shown in the diagram within the border area.

- Each child should then place their feet in the soles and thread the ribbon through the sandals as shown in the diagram.

- You now have a rough and ready pair of play sandals which the children can play with indoors.

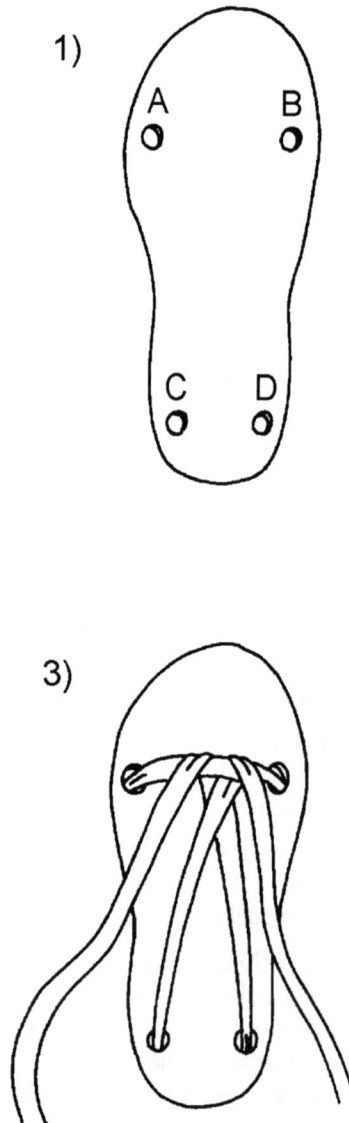

1)

3)

A God who heals

Older children

Remind the children that leprosy can be cured and the disfigurement caused by it can disappear. The children can make a magic slide picture which shows Naaman being cured when he bathed in the River Jordan.

After telling the story point out how Naaman expected Elisha to call on God and wave his hand and cure the disease. Naaman's cure was not what he expected. God cured him and then Naaman was made whole when he recognised God's sovereignty and power.

You will need
overhead transparency sheets
card
scissors
sticky tape
colouring materials
fine permanent marker pens
rulers

2)

4)

1 Cut out a transparency sheet 10.5cm x 14cm. Cut out a sheet of card the same size. On the card draw a picture of Naaman covered in leprosy in the River Jordan. Colour the picture. Put the transparency over the card and tape the horizontal edges together. Trace the outline of the cured Naaman on to the transparency with a marker pen.

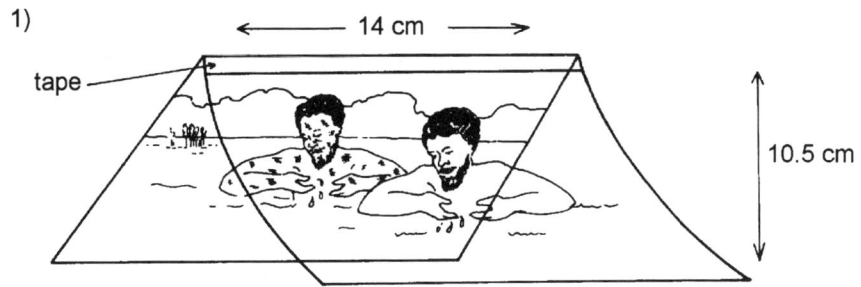

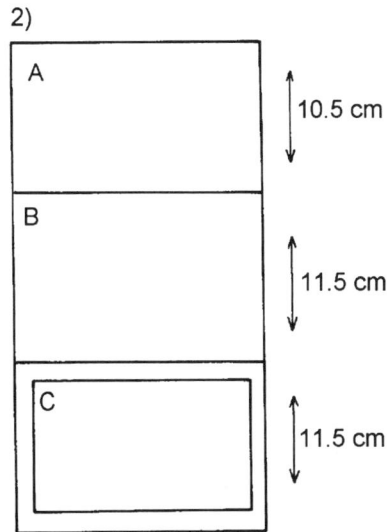

1)

14 cm

tape

10.5 cm

2)

A

B

C

10.5 cm

11.5 cm

11.5 cm

3)

2 Cut a long strip of card 33.5cm x 14cm. Divide it as shown in the diagram. Cut out the centre of the C rectangle as shown to create a 'TV screen'.

3 Fold down A over B and then C over AB. Secure the top of C to the top of AB with tape. Turn the model around so that the taped edge is facing downwards. Carefully slot the drawings into the model, putting the transparency in front of the A card and the 'healed' drawing behind it. The children can now pull their drawing in and out and see Naaman 'being cured'.

WORSHIP
Theme: God's healing action

Prayer: A chain of prayer
Before the session cut strips of paper as for the younger children. Have ready glue and pencils.

When the children come in ask them to write the name of someone who they know who is ill on the piece of paper. Then help them to stick the strips together so that they form a chain.

Father God, through your son Jesus who healed the sick we ask you to help these people in their differing needs; (read out the names on the chain). We thank you that you care for each of them. Amen.

Song suggestions
How sweet the name of Jesus sounds (AMNS122, EH405)
O for a thousand tongues to sing (AMNS125, EH446)
Thine arm, O Lord, in days of old (AMNS285, EH526)
When I needed a neighbour, were you there (AMNS433, CP65, JP275)
Go, tell it on the mountain (CP24, JP65)
Make me a channel of your peace (JP161, SOF135)
Be still and know (JP22)
Oh! Oh! Oh! how good is the Lord (JP180)

Queen Esther
The book of Esther

Themes
Good triumphs over evil
The Esther story shows how good triumphs over evil. The evil Haman at first appears to be succeeding but God's people finally win justice.

Racism
In the Esther story the Jews are foreigners even though Esther is Queen. Haman incites hatred of the 'strange outsiders'. Many children have experienced the feeling of being left out, or ostracised by a larger group. Some children have shown racism themselves and shown discrimination against someone they see as different.

Bible quotation
There is a certain race of people scattered all over your empire and found in every province. They observe customs that are not like those of any other people. Moreover, they do not obey the laws of the empire, so it is not in your best interests to tolerate them.
Esther 3 v8, GNB

The story of Queen Esther, in the Book of Esther, is a story of how good triumphs over evil. It is set in Susa, in Persia, when the Jews were in exile there. Esther, a beautiful Jewish woman, was married to Xerxes, the Persian king. Haman – the 'baddy' – wanted to kill the Jews. He incited hatred against the 'foreign people'. His evil plans appeared to be succeeding, the Jews looked powerless, but then good triumphed. Using their skill and good reputation, God's people confound Haman's plans. God's purpose for his people cannot be defeated. The Jews then lived happily in their adopted country.

ACTIVITIES

Younger children

Good triumphs over evil
Jews celebrate the story of Esther during the festival of Purim in Spring. In the Synagogue the story of Esther is read out and when Haman's name is mentioned people stamp their feet, rattle shakers and boo and hiss. You might like to adapt this.

You will need
card
drawing materials
string or elastic
pea sticks
sticky tape
scissors

- Get the children to make carnival type face masks for the four main characters – the King, Esther, Haman and Mordecai: see illustration.

- Ask each child to wear one mask and walk around the room pretending to be the person they have chosen. The group can then divide into groups of four to act out the story. Get the children to take it in turns to act out the different characters so that they understand the point of view of each character.

- Alternatively make simple cut-out shapes of the main characters from card using the illustrations at the end of this chapter. Cut these out and attach to pea sticks and then perform a puppet show of the story.

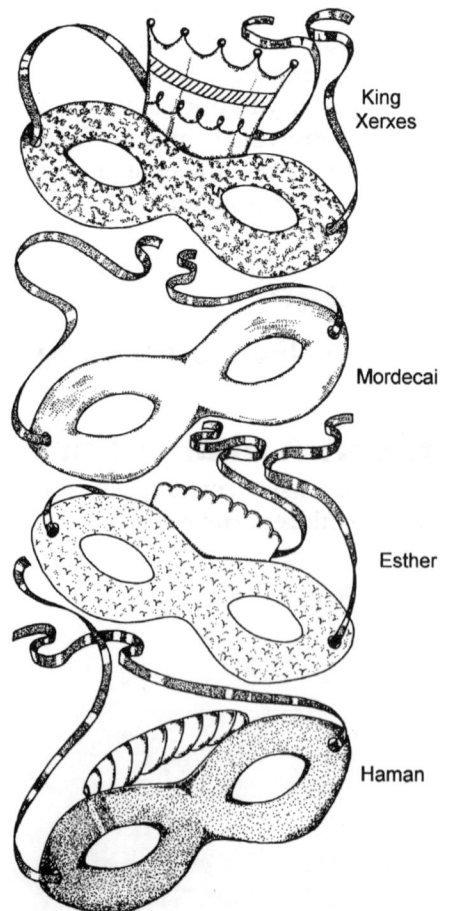

King Xerxes

Mordecai

Esther

Haman

Who profits from evil? Haman's purse biscuits

Older children

People are often seen to profit from their bullying or racism. Esther is a popular story because the success of the evil Haman is shortlived and good triumphs over evil. The shape of these traditional Purim biscuits remind people of the purse that Haman planned to fill with Jewish gold once he had killed all the Jews. But God made sure that Haman didn't profit from his evil ways. God's people became successful. These biscuits remind children of the story.

You will need
125g sugar
2 eggs
100ml oil
300g of flour
1.5 tsp of baking powder
vanilla essence
apricot jam
bowl
tablespoon
balloon whisk
biscuit or scone cutters
egg brush

You will need enough adult supervision for this cooking activity. Ensure that adults are responsible for putting the biscuits in the oven and taking them out again.

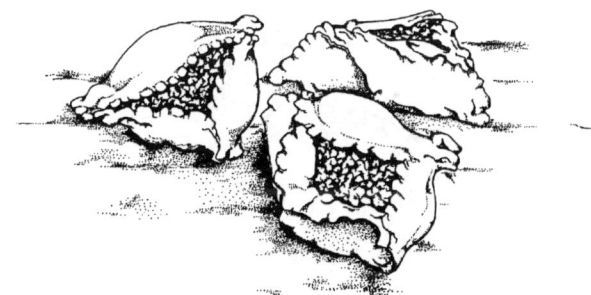

To make the biscuits

- Put the oven on gas mark 4, electric 350°F or 180°C.

- Crack the eggs into a bowl and mix thoroughly.

- Take out a tablespoon of the egg mixture and reserve.

- Whisk the remaining egg mixture until thick and then whisk in the sugar, flour, baking powder, oil and a teaspoonful of vanilla essence to form a dough.

- On a floured surface roll out the dough to 5mm thick.

- Cut out 8cm rounds from the dough using a scone cutter.

- Place a spoonful of jam into the centre of each round.

- Draw up the circle to make a triangle and pinch the edges firmly together. See diagram.

- Beat the tablespoon of the egg mixture and brush the tops of the purses with this.

- Bake in the oven for about half an hour until golden brown.

- Be careful in taking the pastries out of the oven and leave until cool before eating.

Racism

All age

These activities explore discrimination and racism as experienced by children in the group.

You will need
sticky labels
a pen

Drama
Draw from the experience of your own group an incident or a story when a child is a victim of racism, bullying, or some form of discrimination. Choose one incident or story which does not cause anxiety for any child.

Ask the children to act out the incident in pairs taking it in turns to act out both the oppressor and the oppressed.

Discussion
After the drama discuss with the group:

- What did it feel like to be left out?

- What did it feel like to be the oppressor?

- Who are the persecuted groups today?

- Who are the modern equivalent of the Jews in Persia in the story of Esther?

Game
Minority groups in a country are often discriminated against, persecuted or made to feel unwelcome. Older children could play this simple game to help them experience something of the insecurity felt by people who are seen as 'outsiders' in a community.

- In advance of the session write out a set of sticky labels saying – laugh at me – praise me – make fun of my hair – exaggerate the way I walk – whisper about me – joke about me etc.

- In the session stick these labels onto the children's backs so that they cannot see them.

- The children then have to look at the labels on their friends and do what they say.

After the game discuss with the group

- Did they realise what was written on their back?

- How did it feel to know that something was happening to them?
- What did it feel like to be different from the rest?
- Why are different religious groups or certain ethnic groups persecuted today?

WORSHIP
Theme: God triumphs over evil

Prayer
Heavenly Father, help us to stand firm for what is right and to resist what is wrong. Amen.

Song suggestions
Your hand O Lord has guided (JP298)
The joy of the Lord is my strength (JP240)
Father I place into your hands (JP42, SOF31)
Jubilate, everybody (JP145)
One more step along the world I go (CP47, JP188)
When I needed a neighbour
(AMNS433, CP65, JP275)
In Christ there is no east or west (AMNS376)

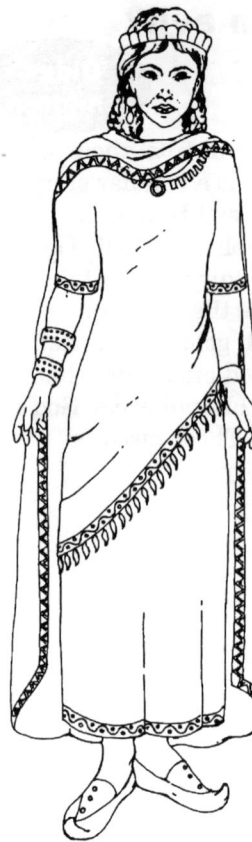
Esther

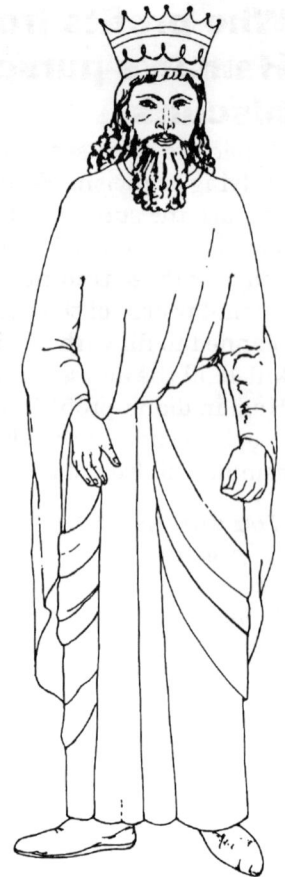
King Xerxes

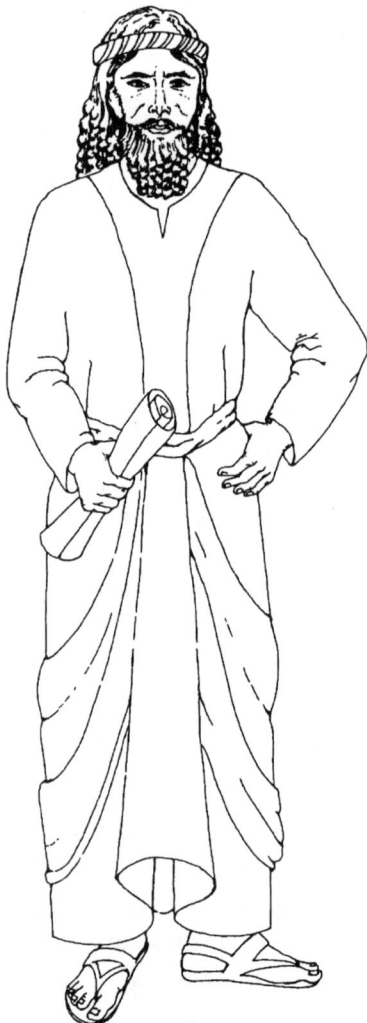
Haman

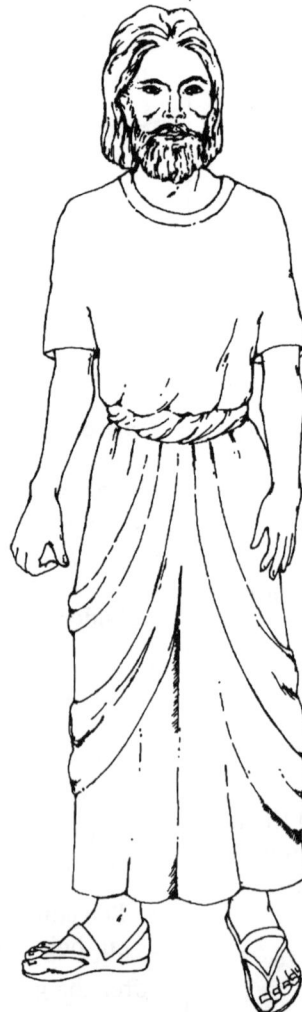
Mordecai

Susian Royal Guard

Isaiah foretells the coming of the Messiah
Isaiah 9 v2-7

Themes

God's kingdom shall bring peace and justice

The prophets believed that the Messiah would herald a new age. In this passage Isaiah prophesies the accession of a king of the house of David. The accession of this new king would bring an end to the imperfections of the present age; the downtrodden would be held high; injustice would end; the sick would be healed and there would be no more war.

Darkness and light

The present age is compared to darkness by the Old Testament prophets. The new age will bring light, joy and rejoicing. The light is a metaphor for the saving action of God.

ASB links

Christmas Day
Years One and Two

Bible quotation

For to us a child is born, to us a son is given; and the government will be upon his shoulder, and his name will be called 'Wonderful Counsellor, Mighty God, Everlasting Father, Prince of Peace'.
Isaiah 9 v6, RSV

Isaiah lived in Jerusalem in the 8th century BC. He was called to be a prophet in the year of Uzziah's death (c.742). God chose Isaiah to tell His people to change from their immoral and irreligious ways. Isaiah warned the people what would happen to them if they failed to obey God's commandments.

In this prophecy Isaiah speaks of the messianic hope. He told them of the accession of a king, an heir to the house of David who would bring salvation and greatness to Israel. In Chapter 9 of Isaiah there is a summing up of this message. The people who have walked in darkness will see a great light. A child will be born and he will govern and be called 'Wonderful Counsellor, Mighty God, Everlasting Father, Prince of Peace'. He will create a kingdom of peace and justice for ever.

Scholars are divided about the passage. Some see it as a post-exilic messianic promise of the coming of a Davidic ruler, others as an accession oracle for the crowning of Hezekiah or Josiah. The New Testament writers believed that Jesus was the Messiah whom the prophet had foretold and so this reading plays a central part in many services during the Advent and Christmas period.

Younger children

ACTIVITIES
Poster making

This activity explores the significance of names of the Messiah given in Isaiah. The children mount the four names given on four posters.

Preparation

On card write the names 'Wonderful Counsellor', 'Mighty God', 'Everlasting Father' and 'Prince of Peace'.

For the posters you will need

sheets of plain wallpaper or large sheets of white card
outlines of letters drawn on old Christmas cards and cut out or letter outlines drawn on a word processor and enlarged
felt-tip pens
scissors
glue
collage materials

Discussion

- Talk with the group about the names they have given their toys or pets. How were they chosen? Are they appropriate? Do they ever change them?

- Ask the children about their names: are any of their names shortened? Do they have nicknames?

- Some of these might have been names given them before they were born. Do they know whether they were called anything before they were born?

Story

Explain that a long time before Jesus was born a man called Isaiah prophesied that a son of God would be born. He used special names to describe this baby. Read out Isaiah 9 v6. Readers in your group may like to follow it in the Bible. Show the names written on card and explain their meanings. Wonderful Counsellor – he will be a wise and just ruler. Mighty God – he will be a divine warrior and have great strength in battle. Everlasting Father – he will be a father for ever looking after his people. Prince of Peace – he will bring peace, prosperity to his people.

Ask the children if they know of any other names given to the Son of God? Jesus, King of Kings, King of the Jews, Son of Man, the Good Shepherd, Christ, Jesus of Nazareth, the Light of the World, Messiah etc.

Making the posters

- Make four posters of the four names given given in Isaiah 9 v6 by using the cut-out letters and sticking them onto the sheets of card or paper.

- Collage materials can be used to decorate the letters.

- The completed posters can then be used in a procession on Christmas Day or during Advent.

Painting candles

Older children

The effect of lighted candles in a dark room provides children with a visual parallel for the opening of Isaiah 9 v2.

You will need
poster paint
washing up liquid
saucers
paint brushes
candles (yellow or white stars on a blue or dark-coloured candle look most effective)
sand tray

Discussion

Read the passage and then explain to the group how Christians believe that the child who will be born is Jesus. Isaiah said the new king would be the light of the world. Ask the children if they understand this. How is Jesus a light to show people the way through darkness?

Can the children see when it is dark and there are no lights? What happens when you turn the light on in a dark room? The darkness Isaiah spoke of is like a dark room filled with people who have no one to lead them and who cannot see where to go. Then light is brought into this dark room by Jesus who guides the people and shows them where to go. The people feel joy inside and they celebrate their salvation.

Candle painting

- Ask each child to spoon a little poster paint into a saucer and mix with water and a drop or two of washing up liquid. It should be like thick cream.

- Stand the candle in a candle holder and being careful not to smudge the paint use the paint brush to paint stars all over the candle.

- When finished leave the paint to dry.

As it will take some time for the candles to dry place a candle already decorated in a tin of sand and darken the room. Read the passage through again. Finish with a prayer.

A dramatic presentation of the reading

All age

In helping to dramatise the reading the children will participate in the joy of the coming of Jesus.

Discuss the meaning of the titles given by Isaiah to the Messiah. Then listen to the relevant part of Handel's oratorio *The Messiah*, 'For unto us a child is born'. After this part there is a section of music which could play in the background while the children do the dramatic reading.

Discuss the passage with the group and then ask them to mime the different verses. Here are some suggestions:

- v2 children walk with eyes covered. Stop and shield eyes from a bright light.

- v3 children bring the harvest in and look happy.

- v4 children take burdens off their shoulders.

- v5 children take off boots and stained clothes and throw them into an imaginary fire.

- v6 children hold a baby in their arms.

- v7 children lift hands up to heaven and kneel or bow low.

Alternatively the group could make a window of light.

Read out verse 2 to the group and discuss with them how they could make a window which depicts this. Follow directions given in the chapter on *Creation* for making a stained glass window picture.

WORSHIP
Theme: A child is born
Light one of the decorated candles.

Prayer
Heavenly Father, we thank you that your son, Jesus was born as Isaiah foretold. Help us to celebrate his birth with joy and thanksgiving Amen.

Song suggestions
From darkness came light (CP29)
O come, O come Emmanuel (AMNS26, EH8)
Hark, the herald-angels sing (AMNS35, EH24, JP69)
O little town of Bethlehem (AMNS40, EH15, JP182)
Awake, awake; fling off the night (AMNS342)
Christ is the world's true light (AMNS346)
It came upon the midnight clear
(AMNS41, EH26, JP116)
Unto us a boy is born (JP263)
Born in the night (JP313)
Jesus, name above all names (SOF112, JP141)
Long ago, prophets knew (AMNS484)

Jeremiah and the potter's wheel
Jeremiah 18, 19

Themes
Acted parables
God illustrated his message to Jeremiah through the work of a potter. Jeremiah in turn told his people God's message by throwing down a pot. Good teachers or preachers often use very visual images to make their point more clearly.

God's people often disobey him
Throughout the Old Testament God chooses holy men and women to remind his people about the sinfulness of their ways. Although God's people had been especially chosen they constantly turned away from their creator.

ASB links
This part of Jeremiah's story is not in the ASB Sunday lectionary but other passages from Jeremiah do form part of the lectionary: Jeremiah 1 v4-10, (Epiphany 2 Year One), Jeremiah 7 v1-11 (Epiphany 4 Year Two, Pentecost 17 Year One), Jeremiah 31 v31-34 (Lent 5 Year Two), Jeremiah 20 v7-11 (Pentecost 13 Year Two), Jeremiah 32 V6-15 (Pentecost 17 Year Two) and Jeremiah 29 v1, 4-14 (Last Sunday after Pentecost Year One). This story of the potter's wheel could be used as an example of Jeremiah's work.

Jeremiah was called to be a prophet in the 13th year of King Josiah (640-609 BC). His call came when he was still a young man. The book that bears his name uses a rich variety of prophetic form: poetry, prose, parable and allegory, to call the people back to God.

One day God told Jeremiah to go to the potter's house. Jeremiah went and watched the potter working the clay. The first pot was spoiled so he reworked the same clay into another pot that was successful. Then Jeremiah received a message from God: 'O house of Israel, can I not do with you as this potter has done? says the Lord. Behold, like clay in the potter's hand, so are you in my hand, O house of Israel.' (Jeremiah 18 v6, RSV). God said that if his people persisted in doing evil they would be destroyed, but if they repented he would build them up. God told Jeremiah to buy a clay jar, to bring together all the priests and wise men, to tell them God's message and then to throw down the jar so that it would break as an example of what would happen to them if they disobeyed God. So Jeremiah did as God commanded. But the people did not listen to Jeremiah.

ACTIVITIES

Younger children

Making pots
By making these pots younger children will be able to appreciate the message of Jeremiah that God had the power to reshape and remould his people.

Discussion
Ask the children whether they have ever made pots? Is it easy to make a pot perfectly the first time? What do they do if it does not turn out right?

Tell the group how Jeremiah used the story of the potter to tell the people that they would have to change and be remoulded by God to be the people God wanted them to be.

If possible take the children to see a potter at work and have a go themselves at making a pot from clay. Small thumb pots can be made from plasticine or salt dough if it is difficult to get a source of prepared clay. Working with clay is very messy and very young children could be disappointed with their results.

You will need
clay
clay tools (or forks, teaspoons, nails)
water
plastic sheeting (bin liners or carrier bags taped to the table to make the pots on and to protect the table)
paint

To make a thumb pot
- Give a lump of clay to each child.

- First make a ball with the clay.

- Then put a thumb in the middle.

- Then by twisting the pot between the thumb and fingers ease and shape the sides of the clay pot upwards.

- Continue to shape the pot without letting the sides get too thin or dry. If necessary use a small amount of water to soften the clay again.

- Do not add extra clay to the pot if it breaks as it will weaken the pot and it will be more likely to crack when dry.

- Using the clay tools make patterns on the outside.

- Leave the pot to dry thoroughly and it can be painted and varnished later.

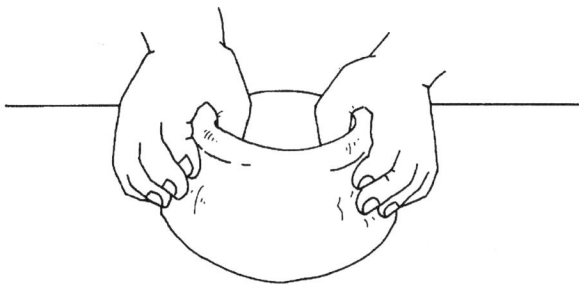

Older children

A Jeremiah pot

In this activity the children will find that pictures or allegories make a point more clearly than words.

You will need: this week
the bottom of a 2 litre lemonade or coke bottle (cut along the line mark on the bottom of the bottle)
newspapers and comics
vaseline
plain paper
wallpaper paste made up in a bucket

You will need: next week
paint
paint brushes
varnish (later, when dry)

Discussion
Jeremiah had visited the potter's house and God told him to throw a pot on the ground to show what would happen to the people if they failed to follow God's ways. The way the Israelites were living was wrong and God wanted them to change. God would only save them from danger if they changed their ways. The people did not change. The Babylonians then invaded their land and took Jerusalem. God often speaks to us through pictures and allegories. Jesus used stories and parables like

The Prodigal Son (Luke 15 v11-32) to describe the relationship between God and his people.

Make a papier mâché pot
The making of this pot is an action parable. The pot is made from lots of broken pieces of newspaper and unwanted rubbish. The children then transform that into something that is whole and beautiful, just as the potter could transform the clay from a faulty pot into a good one.

- Tear the newspapers and comics into small pieces.

- Cover the outside of the bottom half of the bottle with vaseline.

- Dip the torn pieces of newspaper into the bucket of wallpaper paste and stick on to the outside of the bottle.

- Do at least six layers. Alternate the layers with one layer newspaper and one comic so that the children know they have covered everything in each layer.

- Finish with a layer of plain paper.

- Allow to dry and remove the bottle end.

- Paint the inside and outside of the bowl and decorate.

- When dry varnish the pot. Make sure there is enough adult supervision for the varnishing.

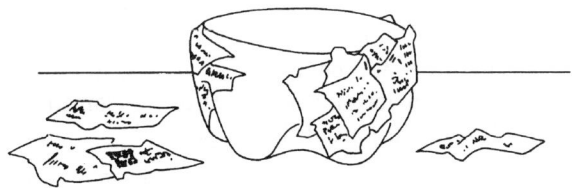

Remaking and shaping 'new life' biscuits

All age

This activity is another action parable. The children take broken sweets and make them into something whole.

You will need careful adult supervision with the hammering and cooking in this activity.

You will need
kitchen scales
baking sheet covered with baking foil
spoon
knife
templates of the pot shape cut from card
cutters which cut shapes from within the pot
hammer
rolling pin

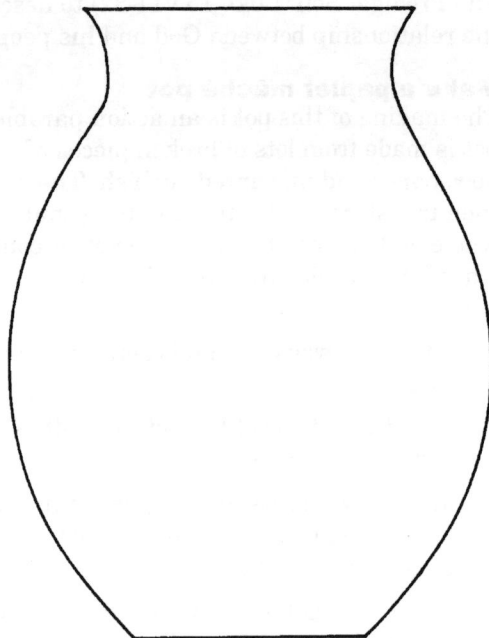

Template

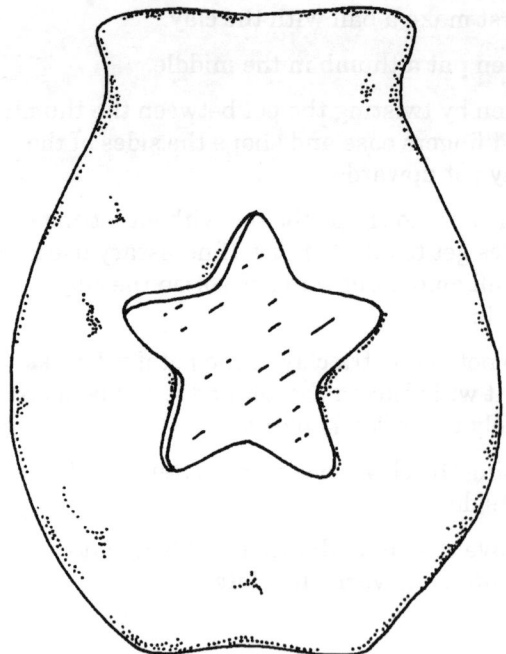

Biscuit

For the biscuits you will need

100g coloured boiled sweets in a polythene bag
225g self-raising flour
85g margarine
85g brown sugar
85g treacle or syrup
2 level teaspoons of ground ginger

Discussion

Tell the story of Jeremiah and explain that the people did not change their ways and Babylon invaded and took Jerusalem. Jeremiah did have a future hope (Jeremiah 31 v31-34) that a new relationship would be made between God and his people. Christians believe that the coming of Jesus is a fulfilment of this hope.

Ask the children to put the boiled sweets in a polythene bag and break them with the hammer. Can they put the sweets together again? Like the pot that Jeremiah threw on the ground it is impossible for us to mend the sweets and put them together as they were. However we can make them into something new and different.

Remind the group that when God sent Jesus he made it possible for people to become whole again and have a right relationship with God.

To make the biscuits

- Mix together the margarine, sugar and syrup until soft and creamy.

- Mix in the flour and ginger. Knead it together.

- Roll out the dough on to a floured board (about 5mm thick).

- Using the knife cut out pot shapes from the template.

- Using a cutter, cut out a shape from inside the pot.

- Lift carefully on to the baking sheet covered in greased foil and space well apart.

- Bake in the middle of the oven (200°C/425°F or gas mark 6) for 5 minutes.

- Carefully remove from the oven and place the boiled sweets in the spaces and bake for 5 minutes until the sweets have melted.

- Carefully peel the biscuits off the sheet when they are cool.

The broken sweets have become like stained glass windows – a beautiful new thing.

WORSHIP
Theme: Changing our ways

Prayer

Father God, help us to see our faults and wrongs and to turn away from them. Forgive us for the things we have done wrong as we forgive those who have done wrong to us. Please write your ways in our hearts and minds that we may always follow you. Amen.

Song suggestions

Father, hear the prayer we offer
(AMNS113, CP71, EH385, JP41)
Spirit of the living God (JP222, SOF161)
Search me, O God (JP212)
Lord of all hopefulness (AMNS394, CP52)

King Nebuchadnezzar's golden statue
Daniel 1-3

Themes
Dreams
Throughout the Old Testament the interpretation of dreams is seen as a God-given gift. God also speaks to people and reveals his message through dreams. When Daniel interprets King Nebuchadnezzar's dream, the King not only understands his dream but recognises the power of Daniel's God.

Idols
Although King Nebuchadnezzar recognises Daniel's God when Daniel interprets his dream he quickly falls back into his idolatrous ways and makes a golden statue that reflects his power and glory rather than God's. Worshipping images, idols, false gods and human achievements is a constant threat to a religious people.

Persecution
Exiles in a foreign land often experience persecution or victimisation. The Babylonians recognised that the Jews had different beliefs and they point out to the King that these foreigners are not worshipping the golden statue.

God's intervention
God intervenes in human history to save his people and to save the faithful. God's presence in the fiery furnace is in the person of the angel.

ASB links
Pentecost 20 Year One

King Nebuchadnezzar II (605-562 BC) was the King of Babylon when the Babylonians ruled over Israel. When the Babylonians seized Jerusalem they took members of the royal family, the nobility and skilled young people to the king's palace. Among this group were Daniel, Shadrach, Meshach and Abednego who were brought up in the court.

King Nebuchadnezzar was troubled by a dream and none of his wise men could interpret it for him. Daniel had a vision which revealed the mystery of the dream. He asked to see the King and told him that only God could reveal the mystery of his dream.

Daniel then told the King the meaning of his dream. The King recognised that Daniel's God was the 'God of gods'. He put Daniel in charge of all the wise men of the land and Shadrach, Meshach and Abednego in charge of provincial affairs.

But the King soon forgot about Daniel's God. He built a huge image of gold and set it up on the plain of Dura. He then assembled all the important people of the land to come to the dedication of the image and demanded that they fall down and worship the statue otherwise they would be killed in a fiery furnace. The Babylonians pointed out to the King that the Jews would not worship the image. The King demanded that Shadrach, Meshach and Abednego be brought before him and they refused to pay homage to the image. They told the King that their God would be able to deliver them from the fiery furnace. The King was furious and ordered that the furnace be heated seven times hotter and the three men be placed in it. But the fire did not burn them. The King saw four men 'walking in the midst of the fire'. The appearance of the fourth person was like 'a son of the gods' (Daniel 3 v25). The King ordered the three men to come out of the fire and they came out unharmed. Nebuchadnezzar recognised the power of God and commanded that no-one should speak against the God of Shadrach, Meshach and Abednego.

ACTIVITIES

Younger children

Golden angels

God's presence in the fiery furnace is in the person of an angel. Children will have come across stories of angels at Christmas and in nursery rhymes. Some young children are comforted by the belief of an angel guarding them at night and protecting them from danger (see Matthew 18 v10).

You will need

outline of angel drawn and cut out from card using the template
PVA glue
spreaders
lentils and pasta
gold spray
paper clips
sticky tape

You will need careful adult supervision when using the lentils and pasta. An adult should use the gold spray.

Discussion

In telling the story of the fiery furnace emphasise how God sent an angel to protect Shadrach, Meshach and Abednego from danger. In Psalm 91 v11 the writer says,

'God will put his angels in charge of you and protect you wherever you go.' (GNB)

Do the children know any other stories of angels in the Bible? E.g. Balaam's donkey (Numbers 22 v22); Samson's birth is foretold by the angel of the Lord (Judges 13 v3); Elijah is fed by an angel (1 Kings 19 v5); Daniel in the lions' den (Daniel 6 v22) and the Christmas story (Matthew 1-2 and Luke 1-2). Angels are also God's messengers. If possible tell a modern angel story.

Throughout Christian art angels have been portrayed in a young human form with with wings. They are often in shining gold or bright colours.

A golden angel collage

- Hand out the angel templates.

- Encourage the children to stick on pasta and lentils so that every space is covered.

- Help them to choose appropriate pieces to make up the face.

- Use pasta twirls for hair.

- When the model is dry an adult can spray it with gold paint.

- Fasten a paper clip with sticky tape on the back so that the angel can be hung up on a wall.

Older children

Worship God alone

Although King Nebuchadnezzar recognised Daniel's God he still practised his old beliefs. In this activity the group explores what it means to worship God alone.

Discussion

Surrounded by many pressures to use our time in different ways people today often find it difficult to worship one God. Like Shadrach, Meshach and Abednego it takes courage to worship God alone.

Discuss with the group what worship is. Use Colossians 3 v16 as a starting point to explain what worship is.

Can the children identify pressures in their own lives which get in the way of worshipping God alone? What are the modern idols or 'golden statues' that get in the way of worshipping God so that God takes second place? Most people at some time or other will find something crowding into their life so that God is in danger of being pushed out. It might be shopping, football or cricket or swimming practice, a pop group craze or computer games. All these things may be good pursuits but not if they get in the way of worshipping God.

Worshipping Nebuchadnezzar's statue is obviously wrong and today obviously dangerous things might include taking drugs, glue sniffing, occult practices and strange religious sects.

A worship song

The group can consider further what it means to worship God by focusing on Psalm 134. It is clearly an evening song and expresses people's relationship to God in worship as a servant. The simplicity of this song can be an inspiration for the children to write their own and do their own actions.

The refrain 'We worship God alone' could be used. Here is a suggestion of what to write.

We worship you almighty God *(raise arms)*
We worship you alone
In your presence we bow before you *(bow)*
We worship you alone
We shout with praise 'Your name be
    hallowed' *(shout)*
We worship you alone.

The song could be read three times, getting louder each time and ending with a loud 'Amen' at the end.

straw

A fiery furnace twister

This paper twister reminds the group how the angel suddenly appears in the fiery furnace.

For each twister you will need
two sheets of card
*copies of the pictures at the beginning of this
    chapter*
a plastic straw
glue
sticky tape
drawing materials

Tell the story of the men in the fiery furnace emphasising the astonishment of King Nebuchadnezzar when he sees the angel appear in the fiery furnace.

To make the twister

- Colour in the two pictures and stick on to the cards.

- Stick the plastic straw down the centre back of one of the cards with sticky tape.

- Glue the back of the other card and stick it over the straw onto the back of the first card. The straw should be sandwiched between the two cards.

- Twist the model by twisting the bottom of the straw. The picture will spin showing the angel suddenly appearing.

WORSHIP

Theme: To worship God alone

Use the worship song the children have done.

Prayer

Heavenly Father, we thank you that you protected Shadrach, Meshach and Abednego. Please give us strength and protection to continue worshipping only you. For you alone O Lord are worthy of our thanks and praise, through Jesus Christ your only son our Lord. Amen.

Song suggestions

I lift my hands (SOF83)
Worship the king (SOF185)
Father, we adore you (JP44, SOF32)
Great is your faithfulness (JP64)
All creatures of our God and king (AMNS105, CP7)
O worship the king all glorious above
(AMNS101, EH466)
Holy, holy, holy! Lord God almighty
(AMNS95, EH162)

Daniel in the lions' den

Daniel 6

Themes

God's power and protection

King Darius was a powerful king but God's power is shown to be more powerful than that of the most important king. God saves Daniel from the evil plots of his enemies and from the fiercest of animals.

Good triumphs over evil

God is in control of the world. The evil plotters against Daniel seem to have caught Daniel out – they catch him worshipping his God. But God has other plans for Daniel and so saves him against all the odds. This leads King Darius to acknowledge Daniel's God.

Faithful courage

Daniel remains faithful to God despite all the difficulties and dangers which are put in his way. He does not renounce God even when it puts him in danger of losing his life.

ASB links

Pentecost 19 Year Two

Bible quotation

He delivers and rescues, he works signs and wonders in heaven and on earth, he who has saved Daniel from the power of the lions.
Daniel 6 v27, RSV

Daniel was taken into exile in Babylon as a boy and grew up in the Babylonian court. When King Darius came to power Daniel became an important official. But the other officials were jealous of Daniel's influence and power and plotted against him. They went to the king and persuaded him to establish a law that no one in his kingdom should worship any god other than the King. Daniel remained faithful to God and continued to worship him. He was caught and put into the lions' den. The King prayed that Daniel's God would deliver him and after a sleepless night he got up to find that Daniel had been saved. This convinced King Darius of the power of Daniel's God. He sent Daniel's plotters and their families to the lions. King Darius then issued an edict which announced that the God of Daniel should be recognised.

Daniel probably lived during the sixth century BC although much of the book of Daniel is likely to have been written later, in the 2nd century BC.

ACTIVITIES

Younger children

Lion masks

Through the telling of the Daniel story the children see how God protects his people from evil.

Discussion

Find out from the children what frightens them. It might be a particular story, thunder and lightning, wild animals or even water. Tell the story of Daniel and the lions. Daniel was brave in a very frightening situation. After telling the story ask the children

- Would they have been brave like Daniel?

- What helped Daniel to be courageous?

You will need

a paper plate for each child,
*   painted yellow with holes for*
*   the eyes cut out, small holes*
*   on each side to thread elastic*
*   through, and a tuck taken as*
*   shown to make the plate*
*   conical*
yellow and orange crêpe paper
*   cut into 2cm strips*
felt-tip pens
glue
spreaders
wool or elastic
scissors

In the session the children

*   Draw a lion face on the plate with felt-tip pens.

*   Cut the strips of crêpe paper into small lengths and stick to the front edge of the plate.

An adult can then thread wool or elastic through the side of the mask and tie to the back of the child's head.

The children can now act out the story of Daniel and the lions using their masks.

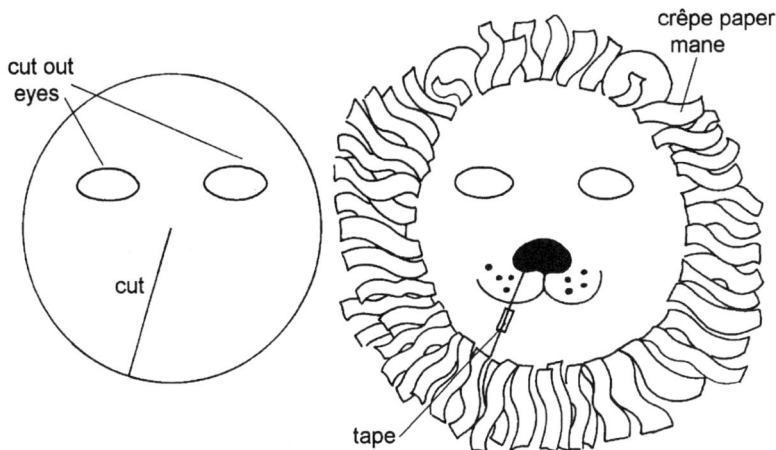

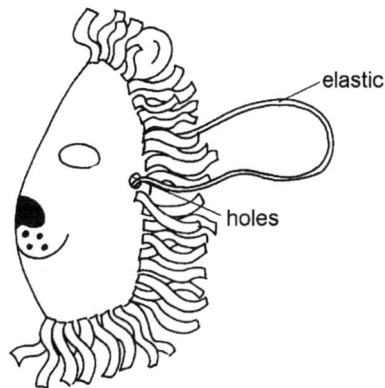

Standing out from the crowd

Older children

Daniel remained faithful to God despite all the difficulties he faced. He worshipped God even when he knew that it could lead to his own death. Standing out from the crowd for what is right is often difficult for people.

Discussion

Ask children to tell each other about times when they have had to stand out from the crowd. Perhaps they were wearing shorts when everyone else was wearing trousers, perhaps a teacher called them out in front of the class or perhaps they could not play football on Sunday because their family went to church.

*   How did they feel in these situations?

*   Did they try to get out of the situation?

Tell the group the story of Daniel and ask them these questions:

*   What do you admire about Daniel?

*   Why did Daniel continue praying?

*   What would they have done?

*   How did God help?

In a small way many people go through 'lions' den experiences' when they stand up for what they believe in.

Activity: A help prayer

You will need
sheets of paper with the word 'HELP' written
*   down the left hand side*
pencils

Ask the children to use each letter to write a prayer e.g.

Heavenly Father,
Everywhere we go we have
Lions' den experiences when someone gets
*   mad with us or puts us down*
Please be with us and protect us as you
*   protected Daniel. Amen.*

Salt dough models

All age

This activity helps children see how brave Daniel was.

These salt dough models take between two and three sessions if the leader makes the dough in advance of the session. Children will need plenty of adult supervision and adults will need to do the baking, varnishing and gluing of the models. Younger children might find making the models difficult but they will enjoy making the lion's mane.

For the dough you will need
4 cups of flour
1 cup of salt
2 tablespoons of oil
about 1.5 cups of water

Mix the ingredients together to make a firm dough. (This quantity makes three lions, an angel and Daniel – so multiply the quantities according to the size of the group.) Keep the dough cool in a sealed plastic bag.

You will also need
baking sheet
silicon paper
card
plate
drawing materials
stapler
foil
paints
old newspaper
rolling pins
knives
garlic press
cocktail sticks
polyurethane varnish
scissors
gold card

All the additions to the basic cone models can be added with a small amount of water.

1   Make five 10cm high cones from card, stapling the edges together as shown. Cover the outside of these with foil.

2   **To make the lions**
Roll out the dough to about 7.5mm thickness. Mould around the cone as shown and press the edges together with a small amount of water. Cut out a circle as shown and attach to the body. Press some dough through a garlic press to make the lion's mane and attach to the head.
Use small pieces of the dough to make the facial features and tail: see diagram.

3   **To make the angel**
Make the main body in the same way as the lion. To make the face flatten a small ball of dough and stick to the top of the cone. Make the eyes by carefully pressing in the tip of a cocktail stick. The hair can be made in the same way as the lion's mane. The wings and halo can be made from gold card and added after the models are complete.

4   **To make Daniel**
Make the main body and the face in the same way as the angel. To make the headcloth roll out a strip of dough and fold around the head, attaching it with water. Add the sleeves and hands.

To cook the models
When the models are complete the adult should put them on a lined

baking sheet and cook in an oven set at its lowest setting. It will take between 5-12 hours. When the models are nearly cooked carefully remove from the oven. Carefully separate the cone from the foil. Remove the cone and then the foil from the figures and return to the oven so that the inside of the model is cooked through. The models are done when they sound hollow when tapped and when you can no longer pierce the surface.

Allow to cool.

To decorate the models the children can paint them and add wings and a halo made from gold card to the angel. Once dry an adult can carefully add varnish. Some groups might then want to make the den to put the models in.

WORSHIP
Theme: Courage
Use the prayer cards in worship.

Song suggestions
Daniel Jazz drama (words by Vachel Lindsay, music arranged by H. Chappell. Published by Novello)
Be bold, be strong (JP14)
Daniel was a man of prayer (JP36)
There once was a man (JP477)
He who would valiant be (CP44, EH402)
Father, hear the prayer we offer
(AMNS113, CP48, EH385, JP41)

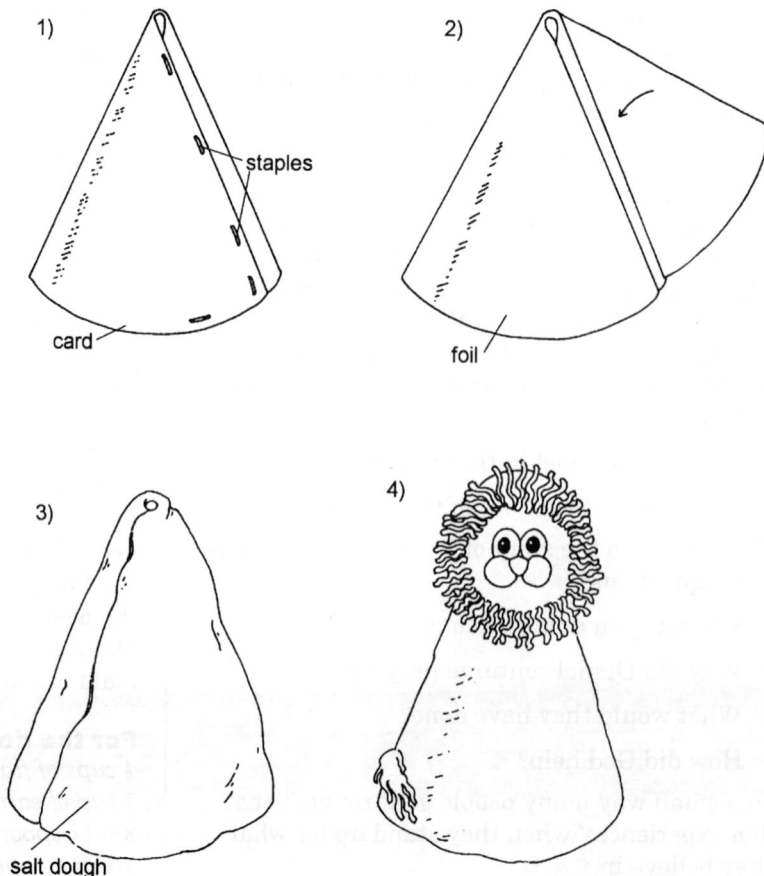

1)

staples

card

2)

foil

3)

salt dough

4)

Jonah and the big fish
Jonah 1-4

Themes
God's providence
The story shows how how God the creator extends his care to all people, even the Assyrians, the enemies of his chosen people.

Obedience
Jonah has a choice whether or not to obey God's command. He disobeys God and his rebellion causes turmoil. But God cares for his people even when they have turned away from him.

Repentance
Jonah recognises he has done wrong and changes his ways. The Ninevites express their sorrow in sackcloth and ashes.

ASB links
The story of Jonah is not in the lectionary for Sundays. As the story shows how God cares for all people, even those who do not follow him, these activities could be used on days when the church focuses on care for the world – Christian Aid Week, One World Week, St Andrewstide (30 November traditionally the time when the church prays for its wider mission).

Bible quotation
The Lord said to him, 'This plant grew up in one night and disappeared the next; you didn't do anything for it, and you didn't make it grow – yet you feel sorry for it! How much more, then, should I have pity on Nineveh, that great city. After all, it has more than 120,000 innocent children in it, as well as many animals!'
Jonah 4 v10-11, GNB

Jonah was a prophet sent by God to Nineveh, the capital of the Assyrian empire. Assyria was Israel's deadly enemy and Jonah was sent to warn the people about the evil of their ways. But Jonah disobeyed God's command and ran away. He took a boat to Tarshish to escape from 'the presence of the Lord'. When a storm broke out the other people in the boat believed that Jonah was responsible for it. They threw him overboard and the storm stopped. God saved Jonah by sending a large fish to swallow him up. For three days Jonah was in the belly of the fish and there he realised his mistake. He 'remembers' the Lord and was given a second chance. Again he is told to go to Nineveh. The people of Nineveh, including the King, hear Jonah, repent of their evil ways and they are spared punishment. Jonah is indignant and angry that God saves Israel's enemies but God shows Jonah how he has concern for all the inhabitants of Nineveh.

In the New Testament Jesus mentions the Jonah story twice, Matthew 12 v39-41 and Luke 11 v29-32. The important point in both is that as Jonah was a sign to the people of Nineveh, so would Jesus be the sign to the people of his generation.

ACTIVITIES
A moving fish model

Younger children

This activity reminds the children that God cares for them wherever they are and however naughty they have been.

You will need
card
scissors
drawing materials
paper fasteners
a plate to draw around

Before the session
Make a simple fish model for each child by drawing a large fish shape with a circle body and cut out. Cut out the mouth of the fish (see illustration on next page). Draw a second circle the size of the body and attach behind the fish shape with a paper fastener.

In the session
Retell the story of Jonah from a children's Bible to the group. Explain that God cared for Jonah and made sure that he did not drown by sending a big fish catch him. Although Jonah had been disobedient, God still loved him and cared for him.

Give each child a fish model and ask them to
- Decorate it.
- Draw a picture of Jonah in the fish's mouth.

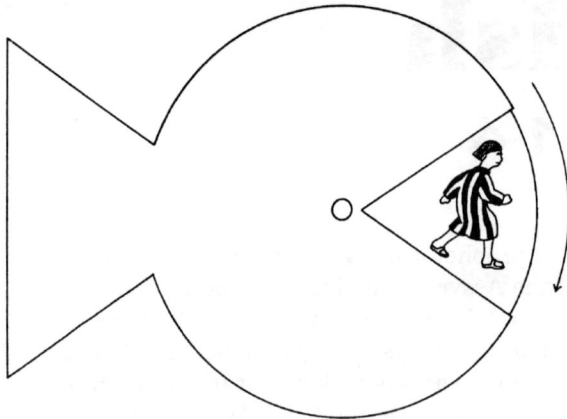

By turning the card circle around, Jonah 'disappears' inside the fish. Remind the children that God cares for Jonah even when he is inside the fish just as he always cares for them wherever they are.

In the belly of the fish

Older children

This activity aims to help children understand the need for repentance. The story of Jonah shows how people need to turn away from wrong-doing, to change their ways and be obedient to God.

You will need
an A4 sheet of card for each child
scissors
drawing materials

To make the model
1 Fold a piece of A4 card in half, and in half again as shown.
2 Unfold. In the bottom half of the card draw the face of the fish as shown with the mouth as indicated. Line AC should be 8cm. Cut this line. Line BD is on the fold of the card. Press the folds of the mouth so that they jut outwards. Lines AB, BC, CD, AD should all be scored. Carefully press along the score lines so that an opening mouth is produced.
3 Fold the card as shown and on the card behind the opening mouth draw a picture of the praying Jonah.

Discussion
After the children have enjoyed playing with their models the leader can discuss the Jonah story with them. What do they think it

felt like to be in the belly of the fish?

In the belly of the fish Jonah turns to God for help. He changes his ways and does as God commands. The people of Nineveh hear Jonah's message and turn away from their old ways. They put on sackcloth, sit in ashes and fast.

Explain that for the powerful and prosperous Ninevites the sackcloth and ashes would have represented a change of heart and a change of lifestyle.

The leader should think of imaginary situations when a child has done something wrong or is disobedient for example:
- broken their brother's favourite toy
- bullied another child at school
- gone to play when when they have been asked to tidy their room

Discuss how the 'naughty' child can 'make good' the situation. How can they say they are sorry and show that they mean it?

Caring for people of the world

All age

The aim of this activity is to focus on the care God provides for all people. It is designed so that children think of people outside their immediate community.

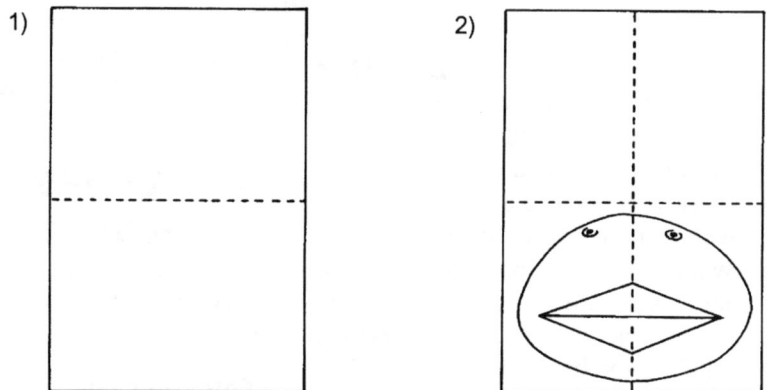

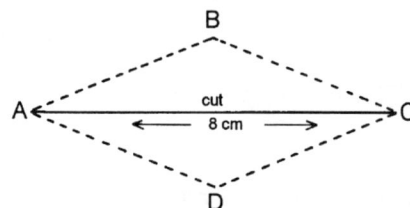

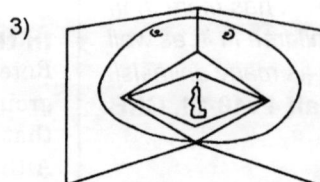

1)

2)

B

A ← cut 8 cm → C

D

3)

Discuss with the group how the story of Jonah shows God's care for the Ninevites, even though they were the enemies of his chosen people. Christians believe that they should show God's care for the world by sharing the world's resources. One way to do this is to have an event or party during Christian Aid Week, One World Week or on a Sunday that focuses on the needs of the world.

You will need
drawing materials
copies of the drawing below to be used as invitation cards

Before the session
The leader needs to make a decision about what sort of event to organise and which charity to support. They also need to check times and book a venue.

Discussion
Involve the children with the planning and preparation of the event to provide an education or fund-raising day for the church.

- Who do the children want to invite?
- Will food be provided? Who will arrange this?
- Will there be games?
- Will there be a time of worship? Who will organise the songs and prayers?
- Will there be a display about the work of a charity?
- Do they want to invite a speaker?

Activity
- Colour in the invitation cards.
- Add the date, time and place of the event.

- Help the children distribute cards in church or ask parents to assist the children to deliver them at home.

WORSHIP
Theme: God is with us wherever we go

Prayer suggestion
Prepare some cut out paper whale/fish shapes and hand them out to the children with a pencil. Ask the children to write where they will be going next week (school, home, swimming, dancing, football, children's club etc) on the whale shape. Collect the completed whale shapes in a basket. Ask the group to think about what they have written and to say a prayer to God about it.

Prayer
Thank you Lord, that you are with us wherever we are. Please protect us in our comings and goings this week. Help us to show your love to everyone we meet, in what we do and say. Amen.

Song suggestions
The Jonah Man Jazz by Michael Hurd (Novello)
He's got the whole wide world in His hands (CP19, JP78)
Come listen to my tale (JP30)
In Christ there is no east or west (AMNS376)
O sinner man (JP194)

HAVE A WHALE OF A TIME

Index to the ASB Sunday Old Testament lectionary readings covered in this book

Many children's church groups base their sessions on the ASB Sunday readings for Holy Communion. The Old Testament readings for these Sundays listed overlap with material in the chapters given.

Has your group enjoyed using
In the Beginning?
If so, try some of these books next!

Festive Allsorts
Ideas for celebrating the Christian year

Nicola Currie

A bumper book packed with suggestions about how to celebrate the saints' and feast days of the Christian year with children. The 58 topics are the best of the first five years of *Allsorts*, the fortnightly children's section in the *Church Times*, edited by Nicola Currie.

£7.95

Seasons, Saints and Sticky Tape
Ideas and activities for celebrating Christian Festivals

Nicola Currie and Jean Thomson

A practical, well-illustrated resource book for church children's groups, primary schools and families, full of tried-and-tested ideas for making Christian festivals fun for children.

£7.95

Be a Church Detective
A young person's guide to old churches

Clive Fewins

An entertaining introduction for 8-14 year-olds to the mysterious secrets of crypts, vaults, graveyards and towers. Packed full of historical information, fact boxes, drawings and cartoons, junior 'church-crawlers' will be hooked for life.

Over 4,000 copies already in print.

£4.95

National Society/Church House Publishing

The National Society
A Christian Voice in Education

The National Society (Church of England) for Promoting Religious Education is a charity which supports all those involved in Christian Education – teachers and school governors, students and parents, clergy and lay people – with the resources of its RE centres, archives, courses, conferences and publications.

Founded in 1811, the Society was chiefly responsible for setting up the nationwide network of Church schools in England and Wales and still provides grants for building projects and legal and administrative advice for headteachers and governors. It now publishes a wide range of books, pamphlets and audio-visual items, and two magazines, *Crosscurrent* and *Together*.

For further details of the Society or a copy of our current resources catalogue, please contact:

The National Society,
Church House,
Great Smith Street,
London
SW1P 3NZ

Telephone: 0171-222 1672
Fax: 0171-233 2592